Books are to be returned on or before
the last date below.

Ref 428

LIBREX–

D0262101

Cassell English Usage

A Handbook of Grammar, Vocabulary and Style

Cassell English Usage

Edited by Tim Storrie and James Matson

CASSELL

Cassell Publishers Limited
Villiers House, 41/47 Strand
London WC2N 5JE, England

First published 1991

**British Library Cataloguing in
Publication Data**
Cassell English usage
  1. English language
  I. Matson, James   II. Storrie, Tim
  1967–
  428

ISBN 0-304-34053-7

Typeset by Litho Link Ltd,
Welshpool, Powys, Wales
Printed and bound in Great Britain by
Mackays of Chatham PLC

Contents

The essay

Précis-writing

Correspondence

Acknowledgments

The writing of this book would not have been possible without the help and encouragement of friends and colleagues. In particular, we should like to acknowledge the contributions of Steven Cook at Cassell, the copy-editor, Pandora Kerr-Frost, Jeremy Dyson, David Swinburne, Chris Harris, Claudia Harrison, Gay Sandford and Rachel Dominy.

TS
JM

London

To Damian in loving memory

Introduction

The History of the English Language

1. An examination of most European and some Asian languages shows that they can be divided into several groups, the members of which resemble one another because they are derived from one original language. Thus English, with German, Dutch, Norwegian, Danish etc., belongs to the *Germanic* group of languages. All of these tongues were developed from a language spoken in prehistoric times by the early Germanic tribes. Similarly, French, Italian, Spanish, Portuguese etc. (called *Romance* languages, because they are derived from the speech of the Romans) are the offspring of Latin, which was one of the Italic family; Irish, Welsh, Scots Gaelic, Manx and Breton belong to the Celtic group; while Russian, Polish, Serbo-Croat etc. belong to the Slavonic group. Not only do the members of any one of these groups of languages exhibit strong resemblances one to another, but members of different groups also show signs of their relationship: European languages even show likenesses to languages of the Indian subcontinent and Iran. These facts have been accounted for by assuming that there existed thousands of years ago a language, called *Indo-European*, which was the common origin of the various groups described above.

2. The relationship of the various languages belonging to the Indo-European family is shown by the following family tree:

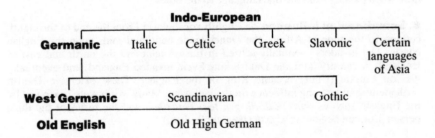

3. The English language was brought to England by the Germanic tribes (Angles, Saxons and Jutes) who settled here in the fifth and sixth centuries. Old English (i.e. the language spoken in England before the Norman Conquest) differed greatly from modern English in pronunciation, vocabulary and grammar: in fact, a passage of English written in the time of King Alfred cannot be understood by a modern reader. Old English, like Latin and Greek, had a complicated system of *inflexions*; that is to say, nouns, pronouns, adjectives, verbs etc. had many different forms according to their grammatical relationship. The vocabulary of the language was almost purely Germanic: very little borrowing from other languages had taken place.

4. English has changed greatly during the past thousand years. Many words have been added by groups of new settlers (notably Danes and Normans). Literary developments and scientific discoveries have been responsible for many borrowings from Latin and Greek. The development of English vocabulary is looked at in more detail below.

5. Latin influence on English vocabulary:
(a) Latin began to influence our language before the Anglo-Saxons arrived in England. The Germanic tribes were in contact with the outposts of Roman civilization, and borrowed a few words, which are still to be found in the different branches of the Germanic group of languages: e.g.

street (Lat. *strata via*); *cheese* (Lat. *caseum*); *mint* (Lat. *moneta).*

(b) When the English tribes came to settle in this country, they came in contact with a people (the Britons) that had for long been part of the Roman Empire. It is probable that the educated population of the British towns spoke a form of Latin. Certainly they used a large number of Latin words, and some of these words passed into the language of the new conquerors. Latin borrowings of this period are distinguished by their form, because the Latin spoken in Britain had undergone considerable modification; e.g.

Chester (Lat. *castra*); *cowl* (Lat. *cucullus*); *provost* (OE *prafost,* Lat. *praepositus*).

(c) In the sixth century, Christianity was reintroduced into England by Roman missionaries. As the new religion spread, the English language adopted a large number of Latin words to express new ideas connected with the faith; e.g.

Pope (Lat. *papa*), *martyr, mass, monk.*

(d) In later times, especially since the Revival of Learning in the sixteenth century (which led to wide study of Latin and Greek literature), Latin words have frequently been borrowed from the literary language. Such words have changed little when passing from the one language to the other.

6. Scandinavian influence on English vocabulary. From the end of the eighth century to the time of Alfred, the Danes made continual raids upon the English coasts. The invaders eventually settled in East Anglia and the north and east of England. A century later the Danish king Svein invaded England, and eventually his son Canute (Cnut) became King of the English. These extensive Danish settlements had a strong influence on the language. Many words were borrowed by the English, such as *skin, skill, ill, get, leg, Thursday,* and the forms of the third person pronoun beginning with *th* (*they, their, them*).

7. French influence on English vocabulary. French influence is indirectly Latin influence, since the French language is derived from Latin; and so a very large proportion of English vocabulary is, either directly or indirectly, of Latin origin.

(a) After the Norman Conquest French, as spoken by the Normans, was the language of the ruling classes in this country, and was also used largely by Englishmen. Moreover, from the thirteenth to the fifteenth century much French literature was translated into English. A large number of French words were thus incorporated in our language. Classified examples are:

   (i)   Words for the flesh of animals used for food: *beef, mutton, veal, pork.* (The names of the living animals – *ox, sheep, calf, pig* – are English.)
  (ii)   Words connected with the household: *master, servant, dinner, banquet.*
 (iii)   Words connected with law, government and property: *court, assize, prison, custom, rent, price.*
  (iv)   Names of titles: *duke, marquis, viscount, baron.*
   (v)   Military terms: *battle, siege, standard, fortress.*

(vi)   Words for the remoter relationships: *uncle, aunt, nephew, niece, cousin.*

(b) The Norman conquerors of England spoke the French dialect of Normandy and Picardy. When the Angevin dynasty came to the throne of England in the twelfth century, the dialect of central France became the language of the Court, and the borrowing of French words continued. Some words were borrowed twice, first from one dialect and then from the other:

> *catch – chase; warden – guardian; wage – gage.*

(c) In the reign of Charles II there was close intimacy between the English and the French courts, and a knowledge of French language and literature was fashionable in England. Many French words thus passed into English, and the process has continued ever since that time:

> *campaign, memoir, prestige.*

8. Greek influence on English vocabulary. The Greek element in the English language is chiefly of modern origin, and is used mainly to express scientific ideas. New words from this source are constantly being introduced because it is very easy to coin words from Greek roots:

> *telegraph, philology, geology, gramophone, cybernetics.*

9. The effect of the mixed nature of the English vocabulary. As an instrument of expression, English has been enormously improved by its borrowings from other languages. It has a greater wealth of synonymous words than most other languages, and is thus more capable of drawing precise and subtle distinctions. Very often we have a choice between a native English word and a synonym of Latin or French origin –

> *almighty – omnipotent; blessing – benediction; bloom – flower; calling – vocation; manly – virile; womanly – feminine.*

In the course of centuries, many of these originally equivalent terms have acquired slightly divergent meanings, and our means of expression have thus been increased.

10. English today is a universal language, spoken not only as a mother-tongue in widespread portions of the globe, but as the official language of other vast areas. It is, moreover, employed as a *lingua franca*, an essential medium of communication, by politicians, scientists, technicians and men of letters of all nations.

Yet beneath the surface of English as a modern *lingua franca* there lies a multitude of differences between the language used by political representatives and international business people, and that spoken by ordinary people in informal or parochial situations. English today continues to enrich itself with words borrowed from foreign cultures. The requirements of the ever-expanding knowledge and culture of mankind have rightly called for new terms to meet needs of expression far removed from those in which the original language developed. With the spread of telecommunications and the emergence of multi-ethnic societies in English-speaking countries, such words have quickly become assimilated and are readily used by native English speakers as part of everyday speech.

Political events in the Middle East are reported in English-language newspapers in phrases which borrow directly from the Arabic, for example *intifada*, meaning uprising (especially of Palestinians in Israel), or *fatwa*, in relation to religious diktats (itself a German word) issued by Muslim leaders, or mullahs, such as the Ayatollah (the leader of Shiite Muslims in Iran).

The assimilation of foreign words is not confined to the sphere of current affairs. The growth in popularity of foreign cuisines in Great Britain, for example, has led to the familiarization of words derived from other European languages, such as *lasagne* (Italian), *wurst* (German), as well as from Chinese (*chow mein*) and Indian languages (*pilau* rice, *nan*).

In addition to its continuing enrichment from foreign sources, the English language is continually being changed from within. In North America, Australia, New Zealand and parts of Africa conditions have arisen over the years that have called for new words to express new directions of thought in terms and phrases particularly adapted to the circumstances. American English, through the worldwide cultural influence of Hollywood films and the adoption of American business practices and terminology across the Western world, has had a considerable impact on mainstream English vocabulary.

Within each country where English is the native tongue there are wide-ranging regional differences in terms not only of accent but also of vocabulary. In the British Isles the verb 'to throw' is rendered variously according to dialect; variants include heave, hain, hull, cop, yack, pelt, scop, swail (see *Survey of English Dialects*, H. Orton).

Fashion sometimes dictates how we speak. Recent years have seen the integration of words and phrases employed by Black communities, to the extent that words such as *bad* (meaning good), *kickin'*, *safe* or *wicked* (as terms of approval) are freely used by young white people. Many of these terms owe much to the influence on street-talk of Black American expressions which have been popularized through jazz and dance music of the post-war years.

Jargon from different quarters is widely and rapidly disseminated in an age of frenzied media activity. New words are coined continuously and buzz-words abound. For example, -isms proliferate in contemporary socio-political parlance — racism, sexism, ageism, Thatcherism — the suffix is infinitely adaptable, having been liberated from traditional duties of expressing systems of thought or established practices, such as Marxism, nepotism, pluralism.

There has been an increase, too, in the flexibility of language, so that users conjoin words to create new concepts. Examples of this are *user-friendly* (used of a machine etc. that is easy to use), *energy-efficiency* (meaning optimum use of energy resources), and *product-placement* (meaning the practice of prominently placing brand-names of products outside the formal setting of an advertisement).

Modern English speakers are also used to the transformation of nouns into verbs to gain a new dimension of meaning; for example, *foreground*, which in its verb-form means to highlight ideas which hitherto have been less obvious; or *fast-track*, meaning to speed up the process of production of a commodity.

What is obvious to modern English speakers is that the language they speak is in a permanent state of change, adding and adapting to the needs of the inhabitants of the contemporary world. And so, the person who wishes to write competent and flexible English has to grasp the essential structure and movement of the language. Attempting to understand the flux in which any living language exists helps people adapt to future linguistic developments and develop their skills in spoken and written English.

A solid grounding in the basic structures of the language is a necessary springboard for anyone aspiring to stylistic flights of fancy. By setting out the rules of English in this volume, the editors mean in no way to restrict or cramp the reader's use of the language. Pedants often forget that the primary purpose of language is self-expression. In most situations meaning is best conveyed in clear, concise and well-structured phrases. A knowledge and application of the rules of grammar is the best guarantee of achieving effective expression of one's ideas.

It is possible for the rules to be broken; but to be broken creatively and with effect, they must first be mastered.

Part One: Grammar

Parts of speech

1. THE NOUN

A noun is the name of a person or a thing. The words italicized in the passage below are nouns.

> It was perhaps a *year* after he moved in with *Ben*, that *Will* awoke in the *night* in a *flurry* of *excitement*. He got up immediately and went to the *word processor* in his *room*, where he typed in the next *paragraph* of his prize-winning *novel* of *love* and *despair*.

We must remember that the term 'a thing' that we use in the definition of a noun includes

a place: Albert Dock, Basra, Glasgow, Mozambique
a quality: truth, happiness, misery
an action: murder, dealing, experience

(a) Classification of nouns

It is not generally necessary to classify nouns, but for the purpose of reference it can be helpful to distinguish the following kinds.

A *common noun* is the name of each thing of a class of things of the same kind.

A *proper noun* is the name of a particular thing, distinguishing it from others of its class.

Thus, *man*, *horse*, *sword*, *computer* are common nouns; but *John*, *Dobbin*, *Excalibur*, *AppleMac* are proper nouns.

Common nouns are of three kinds: concrete nouns, collective nouns, abstract nouns.

A *concrete noun* is the name of something that we can see, hear, touch, smell or taste.

A *collective noun* is the name of a collection of persons or things – band, crowd, host, flock, flotilla, conference, Cabinet.

An *abstract noun* is the name of a quality, state or action – goodness, childhood, maturity, greatness, poverty, flight. If an apple is good, we say that it possesses the quality of goodness. We may abstract this quality, i.e. consider it apart from the thing that possesses it. An abstract noun is thus the name of a mental or philosophical conception.

(b) Nouns and number

A noun or pronoun is said to be in the singular number when it denotes one person or thing. It is said to be in the plural number when it denotes more than one person or thing:

singular: man, woman, child, pen, bus
plural: men, women, children, pens, buses

Nouns form their plurals in several different ways.

(i) By adding -*en* to the singular:

ox, oxen
child, children
brother, brethren

(ii) By a change of vowel:
   mouse, mice
   goose, geese
   tooth, teeth
   louse, lice

(iii) Without change:
   sheep, sheep
   swine, swine
Many such plurals are names of animals, as with: a shoal of cod/trout/salmon etc.
Others need not change, but are not specifically animal-related:
   aircraft, aircraft
   counsel (meaning barrister), counsel
   quid, quid

(iv) By adding -*s* or -*es*:
   boy, boys   ass, asses
   leg, legs   batch, batches
   bus, buses   pass, passes
   craze, crazes   fax, faxes

(v) By changing -*y* to -*ies* after a consonant:
   fly, flies
   lady, ladies

(vi) By adding -*s* to -y after a vowel:
   trolley, trolleys
Note that *money*, *monies* is an exception to this rule.

(vii) By changing -*f(e)* to -*ves*:
   calf, calves
   knife, knives
   shelf, shelves
   wife, wives
Note that some nouns retain -*fs* rather than -*ves*:
   roof, roofs
   belief, beliefs
   cliff, cliffs
   proof, proofs
And some can take either ending:
   dwarf, dwarfs or dwarves
   wharf, wharfs or wharves

(viii) Plurals of words borrowed from other languages
Words borrowed directly from other languages retain their original plurals.

(1) Plurals in -*a*. Latin words with the singular ending -um and Greek words with
the singular ending -on change to -a:
   addendum, addenda
   bacterium, bacteria
   ovum, ova
   criterion, criteria
   phenomenon, phenomena
But some commonly-used words need not revert to their original plural form:
   museum, museums
   stadium, stadia or stadiums

(2) Plurals in -*ae*. Latin words ending in -a take -ae:

    antenna, antennae (insects), antennas (radios)

    larva, larvae

    vertebra, vertebrae

But *drama, dramas* (a Greek word).

(3) Plural in -*i*. Italian words ending in -o take an -i ending:

    virtuoso, virtuosi

Some commonly-used words, such as names of pasta shapes, are always in the plural:

    spaghetti, fusilli, ravioli

Latin words ending in -us often take -i in their plural form:

    alumnus, alumni

    cactus, cacti

    stimulus, stimuli

    nucleus, nuclei

Some commonly-used Latin words ending in -us take a normal -es ending:

    campus, campuses

    chorus, choruses

    virus, viruses

    genius, geniuses (meaning clever person) or genii (meaning familiar spirit)

(4) Plurals of words ending in -*ex* or -*ix*. Latin words ending in -ex or -ix may change to -ices:

    index, indices (when relating to mathematical terms) or indexes (when relating to books)

    matrix, matrices

    vortex, vortices

(5) Plurals of words ending in -*is*. Latin or Greek nouns ending in -is take -es endings:

    analysis, analyses

    axis, axes

    hypothesis, hypotheses

    parenthesis, parentheses

(6) Plurals in -*im*: Hebrew nouns may take the plural ending -im:

    cherub, cherubim (meaning angelic spirit) or cherubs (meaning beautiful child)

    kibbutz, kibbutzim

(7) Plurals in -*aux*. French plurals ending in -au take -x:

    beau, beaux

    château, châteaux

(ix) Plurals of compounds

Compound nouns form their plural by adding -s to the chief word. This is normal when the second element is a noun.

    Girl Guides

    football hooligans

    boy friends

    club-goers

Note the pattern where the compound is made up of a prepositional phrase: only the chief noun (not necessarily the last word) takes the plural form:

    commanders-in-chief

    fathers-in-law

    hangers-on

    men-o'-war

    passers-by

Some hyphenated expressions ending with a noun put that noun into the plural even when it is not the main word:

will-o'-the-wisps

Jack-in-the-boxes

(c) Cases and the noun

A noun or pronoun is said to be in a certain case according to its relationship to other words in the sentence. Thus in the sentence

I gave the *book* to *John.*

I is in the nominative case because it is the subject; *book* is in the accusative case because it is the object. *John* is in the accusative case because it is governed by a preposition.

Explanations of the cases are below.

(i) The nominative case

The nominative is the case of the subject of a sentence or a clause.

John said so.

We know that *children* love play.

(ii) The vocative case

The vocative is used in addressing a person or thing.

Sir! Oy you!

Friends, Romans, Countrymen . . .

(iii) The accusative case

The accusative is the case of:

the object of a sentence or clause:

Cats like *milk.*

Tell me if you meet my *friend.*

a predicative noun referring to the object:

They elected her *president.*

Mike proved him a *liar.*

a noun used after a preposition:

I gave the book to *her.*

I will send the parcel to my *Dad.*

The shoppers passed through the cashiers' *tills.*

nouns used adverbially to indicate measurement of space or time:

I have walked ten *miles.* (Note that *miles* is not the object of the verb; *ten miles* indicates how far I have walked, not what I have walked.)

I waited an *hour* for you.

(iv) The genitive case

The genitive usually denotes the possessor or owner, and is used as an adjective-equivalent qualifying a following noun:

The *boy's* hat; the *boys'* soccer team.

The *bank's* computer print-out.

The genitive singular is formed by adding -*'s* to the nominative:

girl's, lover's, student's

by adding a simple apostrophe to the nominative plural where that ends in -*s* or -*es*:

asses', students'

or by adding -*'s* to the nominative plural if that form does not already end in -*s*:

men's, children's

Note that there are some exceptional cases. Greek and Hebrew words ending in '-*s*' take only an apostrophe for the genitive singular:

Moses' law, *Socrates'* speech

Note also the set phrases *for conscience' sake, for goodness' sake.*

The full genitive form should be used, however, in such expressions as *Dickens's* novels, *Keats's* Odes, in order to make it clear in pronunciation that we are not speaking of the novels of Dicken or the odes of Keat.

The *of* construction. Besides the inflected form of the genitive described above, we may use a phrase beginning with the preposition *of*:

David's son, the son *of David*.

However, it is important to note that although the phrase 'of David' is equivalent to the genitive, 'David' is in the accusative case governed by the preposition *of*.

(v) The dative case

This is the case of the indirect object.

Thus in the sentence, 'I sent *Jones* a fax,' the word *fax* names the thing directly affected by the action of sending, whereas *Jones* names the person indirectly affected by the action. *Fax* is the direct object (accusative case), and *Jones* is the indirect object (dative case). Other examples are:

I gave *Abdul* a call.

John gave the *beggar* a few coppers.

Show your *friend* the picture.

The chemist made the *woman* up some medicine.

(d) Gender

Nouns and pronouns in English, unlike those in many foreign languages (French and Spanish for instance), are not classified into groups of masculine and feminine. However, grammatical gender is evident in the way some nouns can be modified to take account of sex:

man, woman

lion, lioness

bull, heifer

police officer, woman police officer

(e) A note on apposition

A noun, or noun-equivalent, is said to be in apposition to another when it gives fuller definition to the meaning of that other noun or noun-equivalent. Both nouns or noun-equivalents name the same person or thing:

Nicholas, *Tsar of all the Russias*, was overthrown by Lenin. ('Tsar' is in apposition to 'Nicholas'.)

My client, *Mr Smith*, has instructed me to write to you, *the occupant* of the premises. ('Mr Smith' is in apposition to 'my client'. 'The occupant' is in apposition to 'you'.)

A noun-clause may be in apposition to a noun or pronoun:

He gave orders *that all protesters should be arrested*.

The subordinate clause here defines what is meant by *orders*; in effect, it does the work of an adjective qualifying *orders*. It should be understood that the word *that* is not acting as a relative pronoun, but as a subordinating conjunction.

2. THE VERB

A verb is a word that indicates being or doing on the part of the person or thing denoted by the subject of the sentence or clause. Every sentence or clause must contain a verb (expressed or understood) as part of the predicate.

Most verbs denote an action:

She *took* a taxi home.

Most people *like* dogs.

The sun *rises* in the east.

The postman *brings* letters.

Some verbs denote a state:

They *seem* happy.

He *is* the proprietor.

Verbs also denote a change of state:

The boy *became* an artist.

The grocer's daughter *became* prime minister.

Verbs often appear in compound forms:

They *are walking*.

I *do know* this.

He *had gone*.

Were they *missed*?

Will you *have finished* by five o'clock?

The house *had been sold*.

(a) Transitive, intransitive, auxiliary

The basic form of a verb, which expresses simply the notion of the verb without predicating it of any subject, is called the infinitive:

to love, to be, to prosper, to care

Verbs may be divided into three main classes:

(i) Transitive verbs

A transitive verb is one that denotes an action performed directly upon an object:

Jack *built* the house.

Gail *stole* the cheque.

The sense of a transitive verb is not complete without the object.

Only transitive verbs can take the passive voice (see (d) p.7).

(ii) Intransitive verbs

An intransitive verb is one denoting an action that is not performed upon an object:

The horse *runs* swiftly.

He *swam* a mile.

Many verbs may be either transitive or intransitive according to the sentence in which they appear:

Transitive	Intransitive
Frank *strikes* his opponent.	The clock *strikes*.
Ring the bell.	The bell *rings*.
Debbie *grows* house-plants.	Tomatoes *grow* there.

Points to note:

(1) An intransitive verb sometimes takes an object having a meaning closely connected with its own:

Christie *ran* a *race*.

I *have lived* my *life*.

In these cases, *race* and *life* are called cognate objects.

(2) An intransitive verb is sometimes so intimately connected with a following preposition that the verb and preposition may be regarded as forming a transitive compound verb:

He *laughs at* me. (*Me* is the object of the verb *laughs at*.)

I *rely on* your friendship.

Such verbs should be considered transitive only if they can be turned into the passive voice:

I *am laughed at* by him.

(iii) Auxiliary verbs

An auxiliary verb is one that is not used alone, but helps another verb to form a voice, tense or mood:

I *am* driven, I *shall* write, she *may* go.

The auxiliary verbs are:

be, have, do, may, shall, will

(b) Verbs of incomplete predication: transitive and intransitive

Some intransitive verbs do not make complete sense unless they are followed by a predicative adjective or predicative noun or noun-equivalent:

She *seems* ill.

Sanjay soon *became* one of the lads.

This *is* what I expected.

Since they cannot form a complete predicate alone, such verbs are called verbs of incomplete predication.

The chief intransitive verbs of this kind are:

be, seem, become, be made, be supposed, be called, be named

Similarly, some transitive verbs do not make complete sense without a predicative word referring to the object. These are also verbs of incomplete predication:

The government *made* free speech illegal.

The food *made* him ill.

He *pronounced* me fit.

It should be noted that the verb *to be* can never have an object.

(c) Person and number

A verb is conjugated in order to agree with the three 'persons' in singular and plural, as follows –

	singular	plural
1st person	I	we
2nd person	you	you
3rd person	he, she, it	they

A verb agrees with its subject in person and number.

Thus, in 'he goes', both the subject 'he' and the verb 'goes' are in the third person singular.

A verb which is limited by person and number, as is 'he goes' in the above example, is termed a *finite* verb.

(d) Voice: active and passive

Voice is that form of the verb which shows whether the person or thing denoted by the subject acts, or is acted upon. A verb is said to be in the active voice when the person or thing denoted by the subject performs an action:

(1) Pat *posted* the letter.

(2) Florence *ran* the race.

A verb is said to be in the passive voice when the person or thing denoted by the subject undergoes or suffers an action:

(3) The letter *was posted* by Pat.

(4) A great race *was run* by Florence.

It will be seen that the letter, which was the object of the active construction in (1), has become the subject of the passive construction in (3). It follows from this that an active verb cannot be turned into the passive unless it has an object; in other words, only transitive verbs have a passive voice.

There are two points which should be noted.

(i) Verbs that take two direct objects, or a direct and an indirect object, may retain one of the objects in the passive construction:

He *taught* me computer studies. (active)

The manager *offered* Janice the job. (active)

I *was taught* computer studies by him. (passive)
Janice *was offered* the job by the manager. (passive)
'Computer studies' and 'job' in the last two sentences are called retained accusatives by grammarians.

(ii) A few verbs that are active in form are used in a passive sense as verbs of incomplete predication:

The flower *smells* sweet (that is, 'is sweet' when 'is smelt').
The apple *tastes* sour.
This car *drives* well.

(e) Verbs and tenses

Tense is the form of the verb used to express the time of the action, the continuance of the action and the completeness of the action.

The time of the action may be:

present	I see
past	I saw
future	I shall see
future perfective	I will have seen

An action still going on in present or past is indicated by a continuous tense-form. A completed action is expressed in a perfective tense-form.

The table below shows how to conjugate the verb 'to see' in its present and past tenses.

infinitive	to see
infinitive continuous	to be seeing
infinitive perfective	to have seen
infinitive perfective continuous	to have been seeing
present simple	I see, you see, s/he sees, we see, they see
past simple	saw
present continuous	I am seeing, you are seeing, s/he is seeing, we are seeing, they are seeing
present perfective	I have seen, you have seen, s/he has seen, we have seen, they have seen
past perfective	I had seen, you had seen, s/he had seen, we had seen, they had seen
present perfective continuous	I have been seeing, you have been seeing, s/he has been seeing, we have been seeing, they have been seeing
past perfective continuous	I had been seeing, you had been seeing, s/he had been seeing, we had been seeing, they had been seeing

(i) The future

The future can be expressed in a number of ways.

(1) Future simple: I shall/will see.

(2) Future continuous. Will/shall with the infinitive continuous.
I shall/will be seeing.

(3) Be to. A way of expressing future events is to use the expression 'to be to', e.g.
Pavarotti *is to* play the Royal Opera House.
Several rock stars *are to* help in an aid programme for the Third World.

(4) Be going to. This is equivalent to the will/shall form of expressing the future, e.g.

I *am going to* see.
We *are going to* see.

(5) Be about to. This should be used when expressing imminent actions, e.g.
I *am about to* read out the list of successful candidates.
The game *is about to* start.

(6) Future perfective. I will have seen, you will have seen, s/he will have seen, we will have seen, they will have seen.

(7) Future perfective continuous. I will have been seeing, you will have been seeing, s/he will have been seeing, we will have been seeing, they will have been seeing.

(ii) Understanding the future tense

The simple future tense shows that an action is about to take place at some time after the present:
I *shall give up* smoking.
Tom says he *will get* engaged.
We *will fight* them on the beaches.
The future perfective shows that an action will have been completed at some point in the future.
By the end of the first half he *will have had* at least one shot at goal.
I *will have given up* smoking by Christmas.
I *will be engaged* by May and married by September.
It is also used to express understanding of actions completed in the past:
You *will have been able* to try out your French on the day-trip to Dieppe.

(iii) Tenses expressing the conditional

(1) We can express condition by using *will*, joined by a subordinate clause starting with *if* or *unless*:
If I don't take the video back, *I will* have to pay a supplementary charge.
Claudia *will* come on Thursday, *unless* she changes her mind.

(2) To express the sense of the conditional in the past, we can use *would*, also with a subordinate clause starting with *if*, *unless* or *but*.
If you had seen her, *you would* not have recognized her.
I would have decided otherwise, *but* Tim persuaded me to stay.
In expressing the likely possibility or intention of an action we use the future tense (will/shall construction), which is often contracted to the pronoun with -*'ll*:
If you go, *will you* bring back a souvenir?
Are you sitting comfortably? Then *I'll* begin.
The use of *would* instead of *will/shall* lends a sentence a different tone, usually of politeness, but it does not change the sense of possibility or intention:
If you go to the shops, *will you* get me some cornflakes?
Would you be so good as to get me some groceries?

(3) Use of should. The use of *should* also implies condition:
If I were in Venice, I *should* go to the Doge's palace.
If the dry rot *should* spread, call a carpenter.
Should can be used to imply that the condition is less likely:
Should you ever become prime minister, *I shall* emigrate.
Should constructions are often followed by the imperative:
If I *should* die, *think* only this of me . . .
Notice that in the sentence above the use of *should* has eliminated the need to use *if*.

(f) Mood

The various tenses of a verb are grouped according to three moods: the indicative, the imperative and the subjunctive.

(i) The indicative is used in making statements or asking questions:
   She *will divide* up the profits.
   Did you *leave* early?

(ii) The imperative is used for commands or entreaties, in the second person only:
   Give her the book.
   Send a courier to the designer.
   Hear me out!
A form of first person or third person imperative uses *let*:
   Let us discuss this later.
   Let her try doing it that way.

(iii) The subjunctive expresses the non-factual, such as the possible, that which is hoped or wished for, and the likely. It stands in opposition to the indicative, which expresses the factual.

The subjunctive has in spoken English been almost entirely replaced by the indicative. It survives often in archaic, literary or formal expressions, but some of the forms of the subjunctive are different from those of the indicative:

present indicative		present subjunctive	
I am	we are	I be	we be
you are	you are	you be	you be
s/he is	they are	s/he be	they be

past indicative		past subjunctive	
I was	we were	I were	we were
you were	you were	you were	you were
he was	they were	he were	they were

In most verbs only the third person singular present subjunctive differs in form from the indicative:
   s/he sees (indicative)
   s/he see (subjunctive)
   In simple sentences and main clauses, the third person subjunctive expresses a wish or command:
   God *Save* the Queen.
   Praise *be*.
   Deny it who can.
The first person plural subjunctive may also express a command:
   Thither our path lies: *Wind* we up the heights.
   It is used as part of a subordinate noun clause with a verb of wishing:
   I wish I *were* you.
   If I *were* a carpenter, I'd make for you a table.
After an impersonal verb, i.e. a verb having as its subject 'it', the subjunctive is used in an impersonal sense:
   It is important that signatures *be* written clearly.
It is also used in dependent questions and commands:
   They wondered if he *were* the culprit.
   I demand that the hostages *be* released.
   The subjunctive is in evidence in archaic adverb-clauses of time and purpose:
   Give Richard leave to live till Richard *die*.

Ride hard lest the pursuer *overtake* thee.
of concession:
> *Say* what you will, I am determined.
> Though the penalty *be* death, I am not afeared.

of condition:
> If that *were* so, but it is not, I should be annoyed.
> If he *had acted* according to my suggestion, he would not be in his present predicament.
> He looked as if he *were* about to fall.

It is important to note that in cases of open condition, i.e. where nothing is implied with regard to fulfilment or non-fulfilment, the indicative is used:
> *If* it rains, I *shall* not go.
> *If* you do not work harder, you *will* never succeed.

(iv) Subjunctive-equivalents
In many sentences the modal auxiliaries (may, might; shall, should, would) together with an infinitive without 'to', are used as subjunctive-equivalents in expressing commands:
> You *will go* up to your bedroom.
> Passengers *will not stand* forward of the driver.

assumption:
> That *will be* the last time we get a chance to score.
> A knock at the door – that *might be* the milkman.
> The conference centre *will cope* with five hundred delegates.
> The proposals for direct input *will revolutionize* newspaper production.
> Balsa *will be* light enough to fly.

questions or requests:
> *May* I *have* another Bakewell tart?
> *Will* you *join* me in a toast to our hosts?

determination:
> I *will not be* over-ruled.
> I *may not be* so lenient next time.

(g) Infinitives, gerunds and participles
The infinitive (to see, to do, to give etc.) and the gerund (seeing, doing, giving etc.) are used as nouns. Note that the present participle (seeing, doing, giving etc.) has the same form as the gerund but is distinguished by its function.

(i) The infinitive with *to* and the gerund
These have similar uses, though they differ in form; the gerund ends in -ing.
Like ordinary nouns they may be used as subject, as object, or predicatively. In addition, the gerund may be governed by a preposition, and be qualified by an adjective:
> *To type* is a great skill. *Typing* is a good office skill. (as subject)
> I like *to type* my own work. I like *typing* my own work. (as object)
> My main contribution to the office is *to type* work given to me.
> My main contribution is *typing* work given me. (predicatively)
> I spend my time *in typing*. (gerund governed by preposition)
> The office was engaged *in touch-typing*. (gerund qualified by adjective)

(ii) The infinitive without *to*
(1) This is used as object of the verbs can, do, dare, may, must, need, shall, will.
> I *can drive*.
> I *do speak* German.
> He *didn't dare* speak.
> We *may marry*.

(2) as a second object after certain verbs, such as feel, hear, see, make.

I *made* him *go*.

She *heard* the dog *bark*.

(iii) The qualifying infinitive

The infinitive is often used adverbially with a verb, to express purpose, or with an adjective, and it is also used adjectivally with a noun:

We shall have *to have* the windows cleaned. (with verb)

A house *to let*. (with noun)

Lineker is quick *to see* a scoring opportunity. (with adjective)

(iv) The participle

The participle acts like a verb in that it may take an object and be qualified by an adverb:

Revving his motorbike, he sped off.

It may be used adjectivally:

A *bubbling* brook. A *broken* reed. (before a noun)

The negotiators came out *fighting*. (predicatively, referring to subject)

I heard the thunder *rolling* in the distance. (predicatively, referring to the object)

Seeing trouble brewing, I made my excuses and left. (introducing an adjective phrase)

(v) Participles in compound verb-forms

The present participle is used with an auxiliary to make the continuous tense-forms, as shown above (p.8):

I *am working*; I *was working*.

The past participle with an auxiliary gives the perfect tense-forms and the passive voice:

I *have worked*. (perfect tense)

The machine *is worked* by turning this handle. (passive voice)

(vi) Participles in the nominative absolute construction

This special use of the participle is seen in the following sentences:

All efforts having proved fruitless, we decided to call an emergency plumber.

All being well, we will come on Tuesday.

Trading being over, the dealers left the Stock Exchange.

In each of these sentences we have a phrase containing a noun or pronoun and a participle and having no grammatical connection with the rest of the sentence. Such a phrase is said to be absolute, i.e. set free or standing apart, and the noun or pronoun it contains is in the nominative case.

(h) Strong and weak verbs

Verbs are classified according to the changes in form exhibited in what are known as the principal parts, i.e. the present indicative, the past indicative and the past participle.

I talk, I talked, (I have) talked

I ride, I rode, (I have) ridden

Strong verbs are those that form their past tense by change of vowel-sound, and without the addition of a suffix. The past participle is sometimes formed by adding -en, -n or -ne.

Weak verbs are those that form the past tense and past participle by adding -ed, -d or -t, with or without vowel change. Some examples are given opposite; there are more verbs listed in Appendix 3.

present indicative	past indicative	past participle

Verbs with vowel change or suffix in past participle

strong verbs

abide	abode	abode
arise	arose	arisen
begin	began	begun
bear	bore	borne
break	broke	broken
come	came	come
hold	held	held
wind	wound	wound

weak verbs

bend	bent	bent
burn	burnt, burned	burnt

Verbs with vowel-change as well as the addition of a suffix

beseech	besought	besought
bring	brought	brought
cleave	clove, cleft	cloven, cleft
feel	felt	felt
forsake	forsook	forsaken
sell	sold	sold

Verbs originally strong that now have a weak past tense

mow	mowed	mown
sow	sowed	sown

3. THE PRONOUN

A pronoun is a word used in place of a noun. By using a pronoun we avoid repeating a noun:

As soon as my brother met his wife, *he* told *her* the news and *they* came to London.

We may also mention persons or things without actually naming them:

That is *yours*.

Nobody knows much about *him*.

Everything was new.

Only *four* of the members remained.

Pronouns are divided into the following eight classes:

(a) Personal pronouns

Pronouns standing for the person speaking are said to be in the first person: I, me, we, us.

Pronouns standing for the person spoken to are said to be in the second person: you.

Pronouns standing for the person or persons spoken about are in the third person: he, him, she, her, it, one, they, them.

It is important to retain the terms masculine, feminine and neuter in connection with the pronouns he, she, it.

Note some idiomatic uses of the pronoun *it*, e.g. the vague sense:

It is raining.

It may also be used as provisional subject or object (where *it* anticipates the real subject, as here: to do that, to act thus)

It is easy to do that.

He thought *it* degrading to act thus.

(b) Possessive pronouns

1st person: mine, ours

2nd person: yours

3rd person: his, hers, its, theirs

Some examples are:

That is *mine*.

This is *hers*.

Are those things *theirs*?

(c) Emphasizing pronouns

The emphatic forms of the personal pronouns are formed by the addition of the suffix *-self* (singular) and *-selves* (plural).

The Chancellor *himself* was present.

We could not go *ourselves*.

(d) Reflexive pronouns

The emphatic use of the pronouns ending in *-self*, *-selves* must be distinguished from the reflexive use of the same forms of words. Reflexive pronouns are used as the object of a sentence or after prepositions, and denote the same person or thing as the subject:

He hurt *himself*.

Through her cunning, she gained power for *herself*.

(e) Demonstrative pronouns

Demonstrative pronouns point out the person or thing to which they refer. They are: this, that, these, those, such, same.

This is obvious.

What is *that*?

I asked her and she told me the *same*.

He really is a clever young man, although he does not behave as *such*.

(f) Interrogative pronouns

These are used in asking questions. They are: who, whom, whose, which, what.

Who is it?   *What* did he say?

Whose is that?   *Which* is our bus?

(g) Relative pronouns

The relative pronouns are: who (whom, whose), which, that, what, and (sometimes) as and but.

Who indicates persons; *that* indicates persons or things; *which* and *what* indicate things.

He is the only engineer *who* will be remembered.

The woman to *whom* I was speaking was the boss.

John, *whose* racquet skill is good, will do well in tennis.

At the end of the drive was the house, *which* was very beautiful.

This is the house *that* Jack built.

What is done cannot be undone.

A relative pronoun acts both as a conjunction joining two clauses and as a pronoun used as subject, object or after a preposition. It is called relative because it relates to a noun or pronoun, which generally precedes it, and which is called the antecedent.

The antecedents of the relative pronouns in the sentences above are *engineer*, *woman*, *John*, *house* and *house*. In the last sentence 'what' is equivalent in meaning to 'that which'. It is called a compound relative, and contains its antecedent in itself, as in the following sentence.

Try to understand *what* you are learning.

Here 'what' joins the main clause 'Try to understand that . . .' to an adjectival clause qualifying 'that': 'which you are learning'.

Special forms of the relatives are obtained by adding *-ever*, *-soever* to the simple forms. Hence:

whoever, whatsoever, whichever etc.

As is a relative pronoun after the words such and same:

His answer is the *same* as his brother gave.

But is a relative pronoun after a negative:

There is no one *but* hates him.

(h) Continuative and restrictive relative pronouns

The relatives *who* and *which* sometimes introduce a clause in such a way that they may be replaced by *and s/he, and it*. The relative clause continues the sense of the first clause, and the relative pronoun is said to be continuative:

I met your girlfriend, *who* (and she) told me you were in London.

This letter, *which* (and it) was posted a week ago, only just arrived.

Who, which, that can also restrict the application of the antecedent. The following are restrictive pronouns:

I could not find the driver *who* was sent to meet me.

The car *that* won the grand prix was Italian-built.

The book *which* he was studying was too hard for him.

In the first sentence 'who' indicates which driver could not be found. In the second sentence 'that' indicates which car was Italian. In the third sentence 'which' indicates which book was too hard.

Who and *which* may be continuative or restrictive. *That* is always restrictive, but there are three exceptions in which *that* should not be used as the relative pronoun, and *which* should be used:

(1) where the relative is preceded by a preposition:

The airport from *which* we took off was big.

The hotel in *which* we stayed was on the sea.

(2) where the relative is preceded by a demonstrative *that*:

That man has a charm *which* few can resist.

(3) where the relative clause contains a parenthesis:

Some people incorrectly add *-ly* to words *which*, according to idiom, are already adverbial in function.

Omission of restrictive relatives

When a restrictive relative is the object of the verb following it, it may be omitted:

Did I tell you about the weirdo (*whom*) I saw today?

Is this the wine (*that*) you asked me to buy?

But the relative pronoun cannot be omitted if it is the subject of its clause:

The car *that* ran over the man is parked round the corner.

The man *who* was run over has gone to hospital.

(i) Pronouns of number and amount

(i) Numerals (one, two, three etc.)

Only *one* was found.   He gave me *four*.

(ii) Indefinite pronouns denote a vague number or amount: any, all, each, few, much, more, many, little, enough, either, neither, anyone, somebody, everything etc.

(j) Number and case
A relative pronoun agrees in number and person with its antecedent, but it takes its case from the function it performs in the clause or sentence:

This is the woman *whom* you are seeking. (whom = 3rd person singular, accusative case)

Punish me *who* alone am guilty. (who = 1st person singular, nominative case)

Pronouns and the genitive
An apostrophe is never found in the genitive case of a pronoun:

its (not *it's* which is a contraction of *it is), hers* etc.

Note, however, that the genitive of 'one' is 'one's'.

4. THE ADJECTIVE

(a) An adjective is a word used to qualify a noun or pronoun, i.e. to add something to its meaning, and so to restrict its application.

An *interesting* book.   Oh I am *unhappy*!
Sparkling gems.   The bridge is *unsafe*.
Four men stayed.

Adjectives are always used with nouns, unlike pronouns, which are used in place of nouns. They are classified as follows:

(i) Descriptive adjectives are those that describe a person or thing: good, beautiful, useful.

(ii) Possessive adjectives: my, our, your, his, her, its, their.
Note that the corresponding possessive pronouns are:

Pronouns	Adjectives
This is *mine*	This is *my* book
Is that *yours*?	I have found *your* book
He said it was *his*	Have you seen *his* book?

(iii) Emphasizing adjectives: own and very.
I am my *own* boss.
The *very* dogs shunned him.

(iv) Demonstrative adjectives: this, that, these, those, such, same.
He came to *this* town.
What are *those* boxes for?

The demonstrative adjectives agree in number with the nouns they qualify:

This cheese. *Those* cheeses.

Remember that *the* and *a, an* are also demonstrative adjectives known as the definite and indefinite articles respectively.

(v) Interrogative adjectives: what and which.
What answer did she give?
Which way did they go?

(vi) Relative adjectives
Which and *what* are sometimes used with nouns to introduce relative clauses:

Take *which* book you prefer.

He lived through the war-years, during *which* period he learnt about poverty and pain.

Becky used *what* material she possessed.

(b) Adjectives of number and amount

(i) Cardinal numerals:
one boy, *three* men etc.

(ii) Ordinal numerals denoting position in a series:
first place, *second* eleven, *third* man

(iii) Most of the indefinite pronouns may also be used as indefinite adjectives:
Few people were present.
Other people objected.
Each man had his opinion.
Some cats have no tails.

(c) Comparison of adjectives

The simple form of many adjectives undergoes inflexion when we compare one person or thing with others. There are three degrees of comparison:

(i) Absolute
This is the simple form of the adjective:
happy, sad

(ii) Comparative
This is used in comparison between two things or persons:
happier, sadder

(iii) Superlative
This is used when more than two things or persons are being compared:
happiest, saddest

The comparative is usually formed by adding *-er*. The superlative is usually formed by adding *-est*. But adjectives of more than two syllables (and some of two syllables) use *more* and *most* with the absolute form of the adjective:
beautiful, more beautiful, most beautiful

There are some irregular forms:
bad, worse, worst
far, further/farther, furthest/farthest
good, better, best
little, less/lesser, least
many, more, most
much, more, most

5. THE ADVERB

(a) An adverb is a word used to qualify a verb, adjective or other adverb. Adverbs sometimes qualify even prepositions and conjunctions, but never nouns or pronouns.

Adverbs used with verbs:
He came *quickly.*
They ran *fast.*
We, *therefore,* refused to accept.
There he remained. *When* did he go *away*?

Adverbs used with adjectives:
He became *extremely* annoyed.
A *very* lazy boy.

17

Adverbs used with other adverbs:
> He behaved *quite fairly*.
> Why did you go *so far*?

There are two important points to note:

(i) Many adverbs are formed from adjectives by the addition of the suffix -*ly*:
quick, quickly; beautiful, beautifully

(ii) *There* is used idiomatically as an introductory adverb:
> *There* were many people present.
> *There* was a young man from Newcastle.

(b) Simple adverbs

Simple adverbs denote time, place, manner, number, reason, degree etc.:
> She came *late*.
> They were working *quietly there*.
> He has run *away once*, but he will not do *so again*.
> *Therefore*, I shall not agree to the proposal.
> I have *never* seen him *so* angry.

(c) Interrogative adverbs

Interrogative adverbs are used in asking questions. They are where, when, how, why:
> *Where* did you see him?
> *When* will help come?
> *How* are you?
> *Why* do you say that?

(d) Relative adverbs

Relative adverbs resemble pronouns in that they relate to antecedent and also connect two clauses:
> This is the town *where* he lived.
> Tell me the reason *why* you acted like that.
> Summer is the time *when* outdoor games are popular.

In these three sentences the relative adverbs introduce subordinate adjective-clauses. In the following sentence 'where' is a continuative relative:
> He came to London, *where* (and there) he lived for many years.

(e) Comparison of adverbs

Adverbs are compared in a similar way to adjectives:
> fast, faster, fastest
> strangely, more strangely, most strangely

Examples of irregular forms are:
> well, better, best
> far, farther, farthest

(f) Positioning of adverbs

Adverbs usually precede the word they qualify. But in compound tenses the adverb may be placed either immediately after the auxiliary or after the whole verb. The position of the adverb often affects the meaning of the sentence:
> I *only* spoke to him. (I spoke to him, but did not do anything else)
> I spoke *only* to him. (I spoke to him, but to no one else)

6. THE CONJUNCTION

A conjunction is a word used to connect words or groups of words:

John *and* his brother will go.

John *or* Alice will be there.

Career women are on the up *and* up, *but* not in some professions.

Give me a couple of quid *if* you have a heart.

(a) Coordinating conjunctions

Coordinating conjunctions connect words, phrases or clauses that are of equal rank, and are, therefore, independent of one another:

She *and* I cannot agree. (connecting words)

The dog is always to be found in the kitchen *or* in the garden. (connecting phrases)

I argued with him for a long time *but* I could not bring him to my point of view. (connecting coordinate clauses)

Other coordinating conjunctions are: still, yet, so, for, therefore.

(b) Correlative conjunctions are coordinating conjunctions used in pairs, such as:

both . . . and

either . . . or

not only . . . but also

(c) Subordinating conjunctions

Subordinating conjunctions join subordinate noun or adverb clauses to main clauses. Some of the most common are: that, when, since, after, if, unless, how, though, because, as, than, why.

7. THE PREPOSITION

A preposition is a word used with a following noun or pronoun to form an adverb-phrase or an adjective-phrase.

Examples are: in, through, into, of, about, above, across, after, against, along, around, at, before, behind, beneath, beside, between, by, down, during, except, for, from, off, on, over, round, since, till, to, towards, under, underneath, up, upon, with.

8. THE INTERJECTION

An interjection is a word expressing an emotion:

Alas! Ah! Encore! Hurrah! Damn! Shit! Hell! Pooh! Oy!

Syntax

The way we order words to form sentences is known as syntax. It is important to remember that words are not isolated units, but linked to other words through clauses, phrases and other word-groups.

9. THE SENTENCE

A sentence is a group of words that makes complete sense.
A sentence may express:
(1) a statement:
   He was a brave man.
(2) a question:
   Was he a brave man?
(3) a desire – including a command, a request, an entreaty, a wish:
   Do it at once.
   Bring me your finest wines.
   Make her see reason.
   Let us come together as one.
(4) an exclamation:
   How delightful that was!

10. THE TWO PARTS OF A SENTENCE: SUBJECT AND PREDICATE

(a) Every sentence may be divided grammatically into two parts, thus:
   Birds/fly.
   The bank/is open.
   Most of the Eastern Bloc/has rejected communism.
The first part is the word or group of words about which something is said. This is called the *subject*. The second part is the word or group of words that says something about the person or thing denoted by the subject. This is the *predicate*.

(b) In some sentences, especially in commands and exclamations, either the subject or the predicate is not explicitly expressed – though it is understood:
   Come down! (= You come down)
   Stuff the poll tax! (= You should stuff the poll tax)
   Heads! (= Everybody watch their head)

11. A SIMPLE SENTENCE

A simple sentence is one that contains only one subject and one predicate, containing a single finite verb:
   Dogs bark.
   This pizza is cold.
   The beer is good in Yorkshire.
   Have you been to Thailand?
   What hilarious stories he told!
   Listen up!

12. THE SUBJECT-WORD

(1) Many *hands* make light work.
(2) *Most* of the audience enjoyed the concert.

The subject of sentence (1) is 'many hands', but the actual word denoting the thing about which something is said is 'hands'. This ('hands') is therefore the subject-word. Similarly in sentence (2) the subject is 'most of the audience', but the subject-word is 'most'.

In sentence (1) the subject-word is qualified by an adjective: 'hands' agrees with 'many'. In sentence (2) it is qualified by an adjective-phrase: 'of the audience' describes the subject-word.

13. THE OBJECT

An object is the noun or pronoun denoting the person or thing upon which the action denoted by a verb is exerted:

The nurse helped the *pensioner*.
The driver peeped his *horn*.

The object-word may have an adjective or adjective-equivalent attached to it:

The nurse helped the pensioner *lying on the floor*.

The object can be determined by asking the questions 'whom?' or 'what?'. In these cases the interrogative pronoun becomes the object-word:

Whom did the nurse help?
What did the driver do?

An exception is the case of the reflexive pronouns:

I bless *myself*.   It mended *itself*.
She dried *herself*.   They hurt *themselves*.

14. PREDICATIVE WORDS REFERRING TO THE SUBJECT

(a) Adjectives

Adjectives are often placed next to the noun they qualify:

The *electric* typewriter
The *blue* sky

and then they are said to be *epithet adjectives*.

But when they are separated from the noun to which they refer and form part of the predicate, they are called *predicative adjectives*:

Clare seemed *unhappy*.
India is *exotic* and *exciting*.
Billy's goal was *lucky*.

(b) Nouns

Nouns also may be used predicatively:

I am a *salesman*.
She was a *writer*.
They looked a good *team*.
Vanessa became a *councillor*.

It is important to distinguish carefully between a predicative noun and an object. In the sentences above each of the predicative nouns stands for the same person(s) as does the subject. A noun-object denotes a person or thing different from that denoted by the subject.

Margaret became *Prime Minister*. (predicative noun)
The country elected a *government*. (object)

(c) Pronouns

Pronouns are used predicatively, as illustrated below:

It is *I*.
Isn't it *you*?
Who are *they*?

15. PREDICATIVE WORDS REFERRING TO THE OBJECT

In some sentences containing an object the sense is not complete without an additional adjective or noun referring to the object:

The news made *us* (object) *happy* (predicative adjective).
They made *Sophie* (object) *manager* (predicative noun).

16. ADVERBS AND ADVERB-EQUIVALENTS

In the complete analysis of a simple sentence adverbs and adverbial phrases that refer to the verb are placed in a separate category.

17. ANALYSIS OF A SIMPLE SENTENCE

The following examples will indicate how simple sentences should be analysed using the rules we have already discussed.

(1) Some kids are never satisfied.
(2) Liverpool made Dalglish manager.
(3) The bank in the City made all staff redundant.
(4) I did not see the news last night.
(5) Will you fill up the petrol tank immediately?
(6) There weren't many young girls in the club.

Analysis Key:

i   subject-word
ii   adjective or adjective-equivalent
iii verb
iv   adverb or adverb-equivalent
v   object-word
vi   adjective or adjective-equivalent
vii predicative word

i	ii	iii	iv	v	vi	vii
(1) kids	some	are	never			satisfied
(2) Liverpool		made		Dalglish		manager
(3) Bank	(1) The (2) in the City	made			(1) all (2) redun-dant	staff
(4) I		did see	(1) not (2) last night	news	the	
(5) You		will fill	(1) up (2) immedi-ately	petrol tank	the	

(6) Girls	(1) many	were	(1) there
	(2) young		(2) not
			(3) in the club

18. THE CLAUSE

Clauses are groups of words which resemble phrases in doing the work of a single part of speech, but which, unlike phrases, have a subject and predicate of their own. A clause contains its own finite verb; a phrase does not.

We can divide up sentences to reveal the function of each group of words:

(1) I will telephone/when I am ready.

(2) I know/that I am right.

(3) Show me the picture/that you have painted.

In (1) 'when I am ready' answers the question 'when' and therefore qualifies 'will telephone' adverbially.

In (2) 'that I am right' is the object of the verb 'know', and hence used like a noun in the accusative case. It has a subject 'I' and a predicate 'am right'.

In (3) 'that you have painted' is an adjective-clause qualifying 'picture'. Its subject is 'you' and its predicate 'have painted that'.

19. THE SUBORDINATE CLAUSE

The subordinate clause does the work of a noun, an adjective or an adverb and, according to its particular function in the sentence, is classified as a noun-clause, an adjective-clause or an adverb-clause.

(a) Noun-clause

When she will come is uncertain.

Noun-clause used as subject of 'is'.

Tell me *how you know this*.

Noun-clause used as object of 'tell'.

The question is *whether they reached the spot*.

Noun-clause used predicatively.

(b) Adjective-clause

The passer-by *who witnessed the accident* gave full details to the officer.

Adjective-clause qualifying 'passer-by'.

This is the flat *where I live*.

Adjective-clause qualifying 'flat'.

(c) Adverb-clause

If that is true, I'll eat my hat.

Adverb-clause qualifying 'will eat'.

Though I saw it, I doubted it.

Adverb-clause qualifying 'doubted'.

(d) Points to note

We should take note of a few points regarding the examples of clauses above.

(i) Noun-clauses and adverb-clauses are introduced by subordinating conjunctions. In the sentences above these are: when, how, whether, if, though.

(ii) Adjective-clauses are introduced by relative pronouns (e.g. who), or relative adverbs (e.g. where).

(iii) In sentences that include noun-clauses, the part containing the main verb often does not make complete sense. See the first and third sentences with noun-clauses above.

(iv) The connective that introduces a subordinate clause is sometimes omitted:
Sunil said (*that*) he could not work on Saturday.
I think (*that*) she is the girl (*whom*) I saw.

20. NOUN-CLAUSES

A noun may be used as subject, as object, predicatively or in apposition to a noun or pronoun. Similarly, a noun-clause, which does the work of a noun, may be used in any one of these four ways.
That she will come is certain. (as subject)
She told me *that she would come.* (as object)
My view is *that she will come.* (predicatively)
I am convinced in the belief *that she will come.* (in apposition – to 'belief')
It is most unlikely *that she will come.* (in apposition – to the provisional subject *it*)
All noun-clauses are formed out of simple sentences by making them dependent on a verb (or when in apposition, on a noun or pronoun). Because there are four kinds of simple sentences, we have four kinds of noun-clauses: (a) dependent statement, (b) dependent question, (c) dependent desire, (d) dependent exclamation.
The following are examples:

(a) Statement
Simple: No credit will be given to such a bad firm.
Dependent: The manager said *that no credit would be given to such a bad firm.* (object of verb 'said')

(b) Question
Simple: Shall we allow this firm credit?
Dependent: The assistant-manager asked *whether they should allow that firm credit.* (object of verb 'asked')

(c) Desire
Simple: May you both be very happy.
Dependent: *That you may both be very happy* is my fervent hope. (subject of verb 'is')

(d) Exclamation
Simple: How grim the news was!
Dependent: I exclaimed *how grim the news was.* (object of verb 'exclaimed')

21. ADJECTIVE-CLAUSES

Whereas noun-clauses and adverb-clauses are introduced by subordinating conjunctions, or by interrogative pronouns or adverbs, adjective-clauses are introduced by relative pronouns or relative adverbs. It should be noted, however, that the relative pronoun is often omitted when, if expressed, it would be in the accusative case:

That is not the car *(that) I saw outside the pub*.

Similarly, the relative adverb may sometimes be omitted in an adjective-clause:

Was that the time *(when) you slipped on a banana-skin?*

22. ADVERB-CLAUSES

These are of the following kinds:

(a) Time

The conjunctions introducing clauses of time are: after, as, before, till, until, when(ever), while, since.

She arrived *when I had gone*.

While I was setting up the deal, she was on the phone to Sydney.

(b) Place

Please stay *where you are*.

(c) Cause

Because Dan had not come, I returned home.

Since that is your view, I have no more to say.

As she was ill, she could not make it tonight.

(d) Purpose

He hurried *that he might make the midday train*.

She was silent *lest she might be thought to be talkative*.

(e) Result

Such clauses are introduced by *that*, generally preceded by *so* or *such* in the main clause:

The fat man ran so hard *that he was out of breath*.

We ate such an amount *that we were all sick*.

(f) Condition

If that is the case, I am very sorry.

Were I in your position, I should not do that.

I shall not go *unless you will be there*.

(g) Concession

In the subordinate clause a point is 'conceded' or granted.

Although he is poor, he is honest.

Whatever power he may acquire, Simon will never be happy.

While something may be said in her defence, I still think she is to blame.

(h) Comparison

Such clauses are generally introduced by *as* or *than*.

Jane acted *as I expected*. (manner)

It is not *as good as I expected*. (degree)

Mario is *older than Roberto is*. (degree)

We should remember that a clause of comparison is sometimes suppressed after *as* or *than*, so that we have two conjunctions together. Consider the use of *as if, than that, than when* in the following sentences.

The boys spoke *as if* they were ashamed. (as they would have spoken if . . .)

I hope for nothing more *than that* the whole sorry episode be forgotten. (than I desire that . . .)

George looks better *than when* I saw him last. (than he did when . . .)

23. ANALYSIS OF A COMPLEX SENTENCE

We can divide up sentences, like the one below, to show how meaning is fitted together syntactically.

> Because half a dozen so-called fans at one end make the ground ring with their unending abuse, whilst thousands of other fans, standing calmly on the terraces, bandy comments but are not violent, do not imagine that those who make the noise are the real football supporters; that they are many in number; or that, after all, they are other than a few, ignorant, racist and, despite being vociferous, unrepresentative hooligans.

(1) Do not imagine (*main clause*).
(2) Because half a dozen so-called fans at one end make the ground ring with their unending abuse (*adverb-clause qualifying* (1)).
(3) Whilst thousands of other fans, standing calmly on the terraces, bandy comments but are not violent (*adverb-clause of time qualifying 'make' in* (2)).
(4) That those . . . are the real football supporters; that they are many in number; or that, after all, they are other than a few, ignorant, racist and, despite being vociferous, unrepresentative hooligans (*coordinate noun-clauses, objects of* (1)).
(5) Who make the noise (*adjective-clause qualifying 'those' in* (4)).

24. DOUBLE AND MULTIPLE SENTENCES

Some sentences contain two or more clauses that are coordinate, i.e. independent and of equal rank. Such clauses are joined by coordinating conjunctions: and, but, or, not, for.

The following are examples:

God made the country and man made the town.

We worked hard day after day, and gave her all the assistance possible, but even that was not enough to be certain of success.

A sentence containing two coordinate main clauses is called a *double sentence*. A sentence containing more than two coordinate clauses is called a *multiple sentence*.

But a double or multiple sentence may contain a subordinate clause depending on one of the coordinate clauses:

The couple walked all day, and at dusk they reached a village *in which they could be sure of a hot meal and a bed for the night.*

Analysis of a multiple sentence

Go, Joey lad, and tell that lazy brother of yours, that now he knows, when I get angry, I don't stand for cheek!

(1) Go, Joey lad (*main clause*).
(2) tell that lazy brother of yours (*main clause coordinate with* (1)).
(3) that now he knows (*noun-clause object of 'tell' in* (2)).
(4) when I get angry (*adverb-clause of time qualifying 'knows' in* (3)).
(5) I don't stand for cheek (*noun-clause object of 'knows' in* (4)).

25. HOW TO FIND THE MAIN CLAUSE

The first step in analysing a sentence into clauses should always be to find the main clause. The *main clause* states the central fact of the sentence. Thus we can find the main clause when we have considered closely the meaning of a sentence. Consider the following:

As the night was cold and dark, Jane wore an overcoat to keep herself warm.

The central point of the sentence is that Jane wore an overcoat. 'Wore' is the main verb and so 'Jane wore an overcoat to keep herself warm' is the main clause.

After he played so well in today's match, Courtney could rightly claim to be the team's fastest bowler.

The sentence is about Courtney claiming something. The central verb is 'could' and so the main clause is 'Courtney could rightly claim to be the team's fastest bowler'.

26. HOW TO DETERMINE THE NUMBER OF SUBORDINATE CLAUSES

Every clause must contain one and only one verb of full meaning. Hence, when all the verbs in the sentence have been picked out, the number of clauses will correspond to the number of these verbs. Consider the following sentence:

The report said London had serious transport problems but the committee's chair commended plans to extend the Tube, though opposition to further road building was not discussed.

We can divide the sentence into clauses by identifying the verbs which control the clauses:

(1) The report *said*
(2) London *had* serious transport problems
(3) but the committee's chair *commended* plans to extend the Tube,
(4) though opposition to further road building *was* not discussed.

Thus we can see that the two main clauses of the sentence are followed by one subordinate clause each.

27. PHRASES

It is most important to distinguish carefully between phrases and clauses.

The verb-adjectives (participles) and verb-nouns (gerunds and infinitives) *do not* introduce clauses; they introduce phrases. The following are simple sentences in which the groups of words forming phrases are italicized.

Walking though Chinatown, I met Ken. (adjective-equivalent qualifying subject)

I found the twins, *besieged by a trail of eligible young men*. (adjective-equivalent qualifying object)

On entering Parliament, she achieved a certain notoriety. (adverb-equivalent qualifying the verb)

Vaz left early *to catch his train*. (adverb-equivalent qualifying the verb)

It is also important in the process of clausal analysis to remember to include phrases in the clauses to which they belong.

28. SPECIAL POINTS OF DIFFICULTY

(a) Continuative relative pronouns and relative adverbs

These introduce clauses coordinate with the clause containing the antecedent. Thus the following are double sentences:

I called on Sanjay, *who (and he) was very pleased to see me*.

I called at your house, *where (and there) I was very warmly welcomed*.

(b) *It* as provisional subject or object

In many sentences we find *it* used as provisional subject or object followed by a noun-clause in apposition. Examples of this are:

(1) *It* is unlikely that Simon will succeed.

(2) *It*'s a question of class whether or not the present education system succeeds.

(3) We thought *it* odd that they should want to get married.

Sentences (1) and (2) contain noun-clauses in apposition to the subject *it* of the main clause. Sentence (3) contains a noun-clause in apposition to the object *it*.

(c) Noun-clauses in apposition to a noun

It can be difficult to distinguish between a noun-clause in apposition and an adjective-clause, especially when the noun-clause begins with *that*.

The multinational's lawyers held the opinion *that such a course would be illegal*. (noun-clause in apposition to 'opinion')

Environmental pressure groups did not agree with the opinion *that the company held*. (adjective-clause qualifying 'opinion')

A good way of distinguishing between a noun-clause and an adjective-clause is to consider the syntax of the sentence. In the first sentence 'the opinion' and 'that . . . illegal' are both objects of 'held'. The noun can be omitted without losing the sense. Thus

The multinational's lawyers held that such a course would be illegal.

But if we do the same with the other sentence:

Environmental pressure groups did not agree with that the company held?

we lose the sense, because 'that the company held' is not a noun-clause and therefore cannot be the object of 'environmental pressure groups did not agree with'.

(d) What

(i) When *what* occurs as a relative pronoun it should be treated as equal to 'that which'.

Take away *what* you have been given.

Main clause: Take away that . . .

Adjective-clause qualifying 'that': . . . which you have been given.

(ii) But when *what* introduces a dependent question, it should be regarded as an interrogative pronoun, and the subordinate clause should be treated as a noun-clause.

Tell me *what* you mean.

(e) Adverb-clause of result and comparison

Adverb-clauses of result and comparison are preceded by adverbs (e.g. so, as, more) in the main clause. They qualify these adverbs and not the main verb:

The released hostage was so weak that he could scarcely walk. (adverb-clause of result qualifying 'so')

Becky is more of a computer wizard than you are. (adverb-clause of comparison (degree) qualifying 'more')

The subordinate clause is often left incomplete after *as* and *than*, where the meaning of the clause is understood:

I am not *as* tall *as you* (are tall).

Leaded petrol is *less* green *than unleaded* (petrol is green).

29. A NOTE ON SYNTHESIS

In this chapter we have learnt how to analyse the structure of sentences by seeing how the constituent syntactical parts fit together. The opposite process of analysis is synthesis. By building up a long sentence out of a number of briefly-stated facts we can improve our language-use and knowledge of syntax.

Consider how a single sentence may be written using this list of simple sentences below.

Dan loved the outdoors.

He and his friends came from the inner city.

A handful of his friends had joined him on Duke of Edinburgh Gold Award expeditions.

There he learnt his way about in the Cairngorms.

It was a chance for them to enjoy the wilds of the countryside.

Here is one example:

Dan had loved the outdoors ever since he learned his way about as a youngster in the Cairngorms, where he trained for a Duke of Edinburgh Gold Award along with a handful of friends who, coming from the depths of the inner city, enjoyed their chance to escape into the wilds of the British countryside.

Of course we could divide up the facts into two or three sentences, but exercises like the one above give us a better understanding of how sentences fit together, and how word-groups relate to one another.

Common errors in grammar

30. THE AGREEMENT OF THE VERB WITH ITS SUBJECT

(a) Mistakes are caused when plural nouns which intervene between a singular subject and its verb attract the verb to the plural number:

An infamous *collection of pubs*, noted for their unwelcoming atmosphere, *encircle* the dockland estate.

Here 'encircle' is wrong because it agrees with 'pubs'. It should read 'encircles' and agree with 'collection', the subject of the sentence.

(b) Although two singular nouns or pronouns joined by 'and' require a plural verb, a singular noun followed by a phrase introduced by 'with' or 'as well as' takes a singular verb:

Margaret and Neil *were* there.

Kirk, with the whole of his crew, *was* triumphant.

Barnes as well as Beardsley *plays* for Liverpool.

When two singular nouns joined by 'and' denote the same thing the verb must be singular:

The king and conqueror *arrives*.

Here the same person is both a king and a conqueror. If the definite article had been put before 'conqueror' two different persons would have been indicated and the verb would have to be plural. Hence care must be taken with the definite article or other qualifying words that come before a singular noun.

(c) Collective nouns are sometimes treated incorrectly as singular in one part of the sentence and as plural in another part:

The crew *was* now on board and *they* soon busied *themselves* in preparing to sail with the tide.

For correct agreement, either change 'was' to 'were', or change 'they' to 'it', 'themselves' to 'itself'.

(d) A plural noun must have a singular verb when it is the name of some single object, for example a book:

London Fields is the most famous of Martin Amis's novels.

The Sunday Times is one of the biggest-selling broadsheet Sunday newspapers.

(e) In sentences or clauses containing numerals, the use of a singular or plural verb is decided by considering the meaning.

Ten pounds *is* too much.

Four-fifths of the cargo *was* lost.

Two-thirds of the team *were* Scottish.

If number is the principal concern of the phrase, a plural verb must be used:

They are a two-car household.

However, if quantity is the central idea of the sentence, a singular verb is required:

Five *goes* into twenty four times.

(f) A few nouns that are plural in form can take a singular verb:

Here *is* the news.

No news *is* good news.

However, attention must be paid to changes in meaning if a plural verb is introduced.

Politics *was* her chosen career.

Her politics *are* nothing to do with her upbringing.

The politics of discourse *are* too weighty a subject for the pages of a journal like the *Beano*.

(g) In involved sentences a nominative is sometimes left isolated, i.e. it has no finite verb, is not used with a participle in an absolute construction, and is not in apposition to another nominative. The following is an example:

S/he who would deny that government's responsibility toward civil rights legislation, let him/her read these latest revelations about the country's infamous security forces.

Here there is no finite verb for 's/he'.

But the omission of a finite verb, as above, is often found as a device employed for deliberate rhetorical effect. It parallels the use of the vocative of the second person, as in

You, sitting there comfortably in front of the television, when did you last exercise?

(h) Where the verb has two subjects, one singular and the other plural, unless the form of the verb is the same for the singular as for the plural, the two forms must be used.

The garage *has* been broken open and the bikes stolen.

In this example 'has' does duty for 'garage' and 'bikes', but 'bikes' demands a plural verb. We should therefore write

The garage has been broken open and the bikes have been stolen.

31. BOTH PREPOSITIONS AND TRANSITIVE VERBS MUST BE FOLLOWED BY THE ACCUSATIVE CASE

The following sentences are incorrect:

Let you and *I* eat together.

Between you and *I*, I cannot speak a word of Japanese.

Change 'I' to 'me' in both cases.

Who are you referring to?

That is the girl *who* I'll ask to the party tonight.

Change 'who' to 'whom' in both cases.

32. PREDICATIVE PRONOUNS MUST AGREE IN CASE WITH THE WORD TO WHICH THEY REFER

If I were *him*, I would not go.

Change 'him' to 'he'.

Which books are you looking for? These are *them*.

Change 'them' to 'they'.

33. THE AGREEMENT OF THE RELATIVE PRONOUN WITH ITS ANTECEDENT

Several difficulties arise in connection with this rule of syntax.

(a) Sentences like the following often contain errors:

This is one of the most remarkable events that *has* happened this century.

'Has' must be changed to 'have' to agree with its subject 'that', which is plural because its antecedent ('events' and not 'one') is plural.

(b) The following sentence is faulty because the antecedent to the relative is not clearly stated:

At last, after months of hard work, Rosa passed her exams, *which* completely altered her outlook on life.

A relative (here 'which') should not be vaguely attached to a verb. The meaning of the sentence is clearer when written thus:

At last, after months of hard work, Rosa passed her exams, *a fact that* completely altered her outlook on life.

(c) Parenthetical clauses often attract the relative to the wrong case.

Rosa was a girl *whom* we all expected would succeed.

Here 'who' is required as subject to 'would succeed'. The relative has been wrongly regarded as the object of 'expected'.

(d) The use of *and who, and which*

And must not be used before a single relative clause, because a relative pronoun is itself a conjunction. When there are two parallel clauses referring to the same antecedent, the use of *and* is correct.

We drove to a village *having* one small bar and *which* was decorated with vine leaves. (INCORRECT)

We drove to a village *which had* one small bar and *which* was decorated with vine leaves. (CORRECT)

34. EACH, EVERY, EITHER, EVERYBODY, ANYBODY, NOBODY, NONE ETC.

(a) These distributive adjectives and pronouns (so called because they refer to persons or things 'distributed' in lots and taken separately) should, in strict grammar, be followed by verbs, pronouns and adjectives in the singular.

Each person will have *their* own views.

Change 'their' to 'his' or 'her'.

Each woman will have *their* own ideas.

Change 'their' to 'her'.

Nobody will be allowed to express *their* opinion.

Change 'their' to 'his' or 'her'.

Have either of *you* seen my book?

Change 'have' to 'has'.

Every book and magazine *were* in *their* proper place.

Change 'were' to 'was' and 'their' to 'its'.

(b) Sometimes *everybody, everyone, none* are used to convey a strongly plural idea.

We use *everybody* as equivalent to 'all the people' and *none* to 'not any'. In these cases plural words referring to the distributive pronouns are permitted.

The members of the cooperative *were* enthusiastic for the new project and *everyone* seemed determined to do *their* best to make it a success.

There are half-a-dozen used cars on offer, but *none are* any good.

(c) The genitive case of the indefinite pronoun 'one' is 'one's'. It is incorrect to employ anything other than 'one's' in relation to 'one'.

One is proud of *his* own success. (INCORRECT)

One is proud of *one's* own success. (CORRECT)

35. EACH OTHER, ONE ANOTHER, EITHER, ANY

Each other and *either* are used of two things:

As mother and son left *each other* they kissed each other.

The choice was simple; *either* the blue coat or the green hat.

One another and *any* are used of more than two things:

When the family met they kissed *one another*.

The choice was not so easy. She could have *any* of the clothes in the shop.

36. LIKE

Like must never be used as a conjunction. It is incorrect to say

Vicky does not work *like* her sister did.

The government do not care for the ordinary people *like* the previous government used to.

Other constructions, such as 'in the way/manner that', 'just as', should be employed in place of 'like'.

37. THAN

(a) *Than* is most commonly a conjunction, and not a preposition, though the verb in the clause that it introduces is often suppressed.

Error in the case of the pronoun following *than* frequently occurs. This error may be avoided by completing the clause to which the pronoun belongs –

She has been more successful *than me*. (INCORRECT)

She has been more successful *than I*. (CORRECT)

One exception to the above rule is exemplified in the following sentence:

She likes my brother more *than me*.

The meaning of this sentence is that she likes my brother more than she likes me. If this is the meaning intended, the sentence is correct.

However, the sentence can be read a different way. If the meaning is that she likes my brother more than I like my brother, then the sentence is wrong and it should be reworded thus:

She likes my brother more *than I*. (i.e. more than I like my brother)

(b) *But* must never be used for *than* or *when*.

Ben had hardly been out of college five minutes *but* the banks were offering him work.

Change 'but' to 'when'.

No sooner had I said the words *but* I knew that my accent had betrayed me.

In this case use 'than' instead of 'but' (following the comparative 'sooner').

(c) *Than* is the only word that may be used after 'other' for separating a thing from a class.

None *other than* Rolls Royce could have made such a car.

When the word following 'other' does not separate a thing from a class the word *than* must not be used. Compare the following sentences:

Other means *than that* must be employed.

Other means *besides that* must be employed.

The first sentence demands different means; the second demands additional means.

38. THE UNRELATED PARTICIPLE

(a) A participle must not be unrelated or falsely related.

This follows from the nature of a participle, which is a 'verb-adjective'. Since it is an adjective it must qualify a noun or pronoun.

In the following sentence the participle does not refer to any noun or pronoun.

Entering Florence from the north, the Duomo soon comes into view.

The sentence should be rewritten to provide the adjective with a pronoun to qualify.

Entering Florence from the north, *we can* soon see the Duomo.

As one enters Florence from the north, the Duomo soon comes into view.

(b) It should be noted that in the nominative absolute construction the participle relates to the noun or pronoun in its phrase, though the phrase as a whole has no grammatical connection with the rest of the sentence.

The evening being so fine, we went for a drink to a country pub.

In the following form the sentence would contain an unrelated participle and would be *incorrect*.

Being a fine evening, we went for a drink to a country pub.

(c) In current usage it is now by custom permissible to use certain participles even when they have no subject in the sentence. Some examples are: considering, judging, including, regarding, concerning. Such words are now used with the force of prepositions, as in the following sentences.

Considering the circumstances, the lad had a good game at centre-back.

Judging from what's been said, the firm's relocation to Aberdeen was a good move.

39. THE GERUND

(a) The gerund 'verb-noun' must not be used so that its implied subject differs from the subject of the sentence, unless, of course, it is qualified by a possessive adjective.

On writing to the bank, I discovered I had no stamps left. (INCORRECT)

On my writing to the bank, I discovered I had no stamps left. (CORRECT)

The sentence may be rewritten to avoid the use of the gerund.

When I wrote to the bank I discovered I had no stamps left. (CORRECT)

(b) When the verb-noun, or gerund, ending '-ing' is preceded by 'the' it must be followed by 'of'. In this construction the '-ing' form has no verbal function and is sometimes called a verbal noun. Like an ordinary noun it may be qualified by an adjective.

The careful recording of the band's gig led to a record deal with EMI.

By recording the band's gig carefully the kids made a demo-tape which they could send to record companies.

In the first sentence, 'recording' is a pure noun. It is a nominative with the finite verb 'led' and is qualified by an adjective. 'Gig' is governed by the preposition 'of', and not by 'recording'.

In the second sentence, 'recording' is a verb. It has 'gig' for an object and is qualified by an adverb. It is also a noun, however, and is governed by the preposition 'by'.

40. CONFUSION OF GERUND AND PRESENT PARTICIPLE

(a) Such a sentence as

You must forbid *him leaving*

is obviously wrong. As the statement stands, the object of the verb is 'him', qualified by the present participle 'leaving'. But what is forbidden is not 'him' but 'leaving'.

The *correct* form is to use the gerund qualified by the possessive adjective 'his'.

You must forbid *his leaving*.

(b) A similar confusion of the participle and the gerund occurs in such sentences as

The company's future depends on *the management having the resources* to pay for research and development.

The *correct* form should read: '. . . on the management's having . . .' so that the preposition 'on' governs the gerund 'having'.

No such alteration is possible with the gerund 'being'. The sentence, 'There is no likelihood of *this being true*', cannot be rewritten in the same way as the previous sentence. But today many people regard the usage shown in these sentences as permissible, on the grounds that the confused gerund-participle is now a well-established idiom. In other words, the preposition is viewed as governing the whole of the phrases

the-management-having-resources

this-being-true.

41. THE INFINITIVE

(a) The perfect infinitive is sometimes used unnecessarily in sentences in which an uncompleted action is implied:

I should have liked *to have been* present at Parliament yesterday.

Here 'to have been' should be changed to 'to be' because the idea of incompletion is already implied in the preceding verb 'should have liked'.

(b) The sentence

I intended *to have written* to him.

is meaningless because 'to have written' implies an action which has been performed prior to the action expressed by the main verb. The correct form is:

I intented *to write* to him.

(c) The perfect infinitive is commonly used after verbs, as above, to express ideas of hope or intention. This is part of a commonly-accepted idiom which conveys the idea of the non-fulfilment of a hope or intention.

42. THE SPLIT INFINITIVE

(a) Separating 'to' from the verb through the insertion of an adverb or phrase is known as 'splitting the infinitive'. This is regarded as a solecism in formal writing and should be avoided.

Lengthy insertions in the infinitive, as below, separate the subject from the verb, and so render the meaning unclear.

The poll tax was meant *to wholeheartedly, entirely and at one clean sweep change* the way local government was financed.

(b) However, many forms of the split infinitive, now idiomatic, do little to obscure meaning:

To boldly go where no man has gone before.

The money Sir John gave Steve was enough *to more than make up* for any loss of work.

(c) It is wholly permissible to insert words elsewhere in infinitive phrases than immediately after 'to', e.g.

To have boldly *gone.*
To be thoroughly *recommended.*

43. OTHER IN COMPARISON

Other must be used after a comparative adjective, but not after a superlative.

Gorbachev is braver *than any other* Russian leader.

Here *other* is necessary after 'any', because the class 'Russian leader' would include Gorbachev, and he could not be braver than himself.

Gorbachev is *the bravest of all Russian leaders.*

Here *other* is unnecessary. By using *other* we would exclude Gorbachev from the class of people above whom we wish to exalt him.

44. ALSO

Also should not be used as a conjunction. It is an adverb and is wrongly used after a comma instead of 'and' or 'as well as'.

I was annoyed at doing badly, *also* Sarah's gloating put my back up. (INCORRECT)
I was annoyed at doing badly *and* Sarah's gloating *also* put my back up. (CORRECT)

45. SAME

The use of *same* as a pronoun for purposes of brevity should be avoided.

We received the goods this morning and thank you *for same*. (INCORRECT)
Here 'same' means 'them'.

You are acquainted with the rule and I should be glad if you would observe the *same*. (INCORRECT)
Here 'same' means 'it'.

46. ELLIPSIS

(a) Omission of words necessary to complete the grammatical construction is best avoided as it may obscure the meaning.

Locals *have* and still *do disagree* about the Channel tunnel. (INCORRECT)
'Disagree' cannot follow both 'have' and 'do'.
Locals *have disagreed* and still *do disagree* about the Channel tunnel. (CORRECT)
This is *as good or perhaps better than* the last wine. (INCORRECT)
This is *as good as or perhaps better than* the last wine. (CORRECT)

(b) Often a demonstrative pronoun is incorrectly omitted.

The talents of the father *and the son were similar*.
This should be written:
The talents of the father *and those of the son were similar*.
Note: Here 'those' is used to avoid the repetition of 'talents'.

(c) Ellipsis occurs in certain situations in order to convey meaning briefly and explicitly, for example, the notice at the front of a bus:
Sorry not in service

(d) Ellipsis is not in itself wrong. Many good sentences both in speech and writing successfully adopt an elliptical style for effect. Leaving words to be understood becomes a danger only when it leads to ambiguity or uncertainty of meaning.

47. THE SUPERLATIVE

The superlative form should not be used in speaking of two persons or things.

Rebecca is *the prettiest* of the two.

Change 'prettiest' to 'prettier'.

Lineker is the *most able* of the two strikers.

Change 'most' to 'more'.

48. LAY—LIE

The parts of the intransitive verb 'to lie' ('I lie down'), and the transitive verb 'to lay' ('I lay the book on the table'), are sometimes confused.

Their principal parts are set out below.

Present	Past	Past Participle
I lie	I lay	(I have) lain
I lay	I laid	(I have) laid

49. SHALL—WILL

(a) Very often 'will' ('would') is wrongly used instead of 'shall' ('should') in the first person, when the idea of an immediate future is to be expressed:

I am afraid I *will* not be able to come.

Change 'will' to 'shall'.

(b) When 'shall' (or 'will') is used in a main clause, 'shall' (or 'will') should appear in the subordinate clause:

If you *will* come, I *shall* be happy.

(c) Similarly 'should' ('would') should be followed by 'should' ('would'):

I *would* be glad, if you *should* come.

(d) 'Would' can also be used in conditional clauses, but the meaning is of course different from that of 'should', as volition is implied:

If he *would* bother to try, he *would* understand.

50. CONFUSION OF TWO CONSTRUCTIONS

(a) *I then further remarked* that Northern Trucks Ltd having gone bust, *how could he believe* in the possibility of a take-over bid?

The two constructions confused are:

I remarked that he could not believe . . .

I asked how he could believe . . .

(b) He was particularly glad to note the success the council had in its road safety campaign amongst the city's school children, and also that no fewer than 7000 of Newcastle's drivers voluntarily enrolled themselves to endeavour to go through a year without a single accident.

This might be rewritten in two ways:

He was glad to note the success . . . and also the fact that . . .

or

He was glad to note that the council had been so successful . . . and also that . . .

(c) *She cannot help but derive* benefit from the long holiday.
This confuses two idioms:

She cannot help deriving . . .

She cannot but derive . . .

(d) Substitute for, replace by
These idioms are often confused. 'Substitute' must not be followed by 'by'. Say either:

Machine A has been *replaced by* machine B.

or

Machine B has been *substituted for* machine A.

(e) Due to, Owing to

The uses of these are frequently misunderstood. *Due* is an adjective and must therefore qualify a noun or pronoun, e.g.

The rent is *due*.

He was *due* to take his turn.

In the following sentence the compound preposition *owing to* is required to govern the noun that follows.

Due to unforeseen circumstances there will be no play today. (INCORRECT)

Owing to unforeseen circumstances, there will be no play today. (CORRECT)

The untidy appearance of the garden was *owing to* the owner's absence. (INCORRECT)

The untidy appearance of the garden was *due to* the owner's absence. (CORRECT)

Due to is generally used when *due* is a predicative adjective after the verb 'to be'.

(f) The deliberations of great politicians are like those of great rivers, *whose* course everyone beholds, but *their* springs have been seen by few.
This sentence mixes the relative pronoun and possessive adjective. Change 'their' to 'whose'.

51. WRONG SEQUENCE OF WORDS

Errors sometimes arise through failure to use the right conjunction or preposition after certain words.

(a) *Scarcely* had Jane arrived *than* all the visitors departed.
Here use either 'scarcely . . . when' or 'no sooner . . . than'.

The President now holds *different* views on Russia *than he did* ten years ago.
Here use 'different . . . from those he held . . .'

(b) 'Without' and 'except' are often used as conjunctions where 'unless' is the correct word:

The car will not start *without* (or *except*) he turns the key. (INCORRECT)

The car will not start *unless* he turns the key. (CORRECT)

52. CORRELATIVE CONJUNCTIONS

These are conjunctions that go in pairs, for example either . . . or, not only . . . but also, not . . . but, both . . . and, neither . . . nor.

The simple rule to be followed in the use of them is that each member of a pair should be placed before the same part of speech or kind of phrase, e.g.

This is *not* a fiction, *but* a hard fact.

The following are examples of the wrong placing of various correlative conjunctions:

He is anxious *not only* to acquire money, *but also* eager to display it. (INCORRECT)

He is *not only* anxious to acquire money, *but also* eager to display it. (CORRECT)

Either the action was just *or* unjust. (INCORRECT)

The action was *either* just *or* unjust. (CORRECT)

Exhausted *both* in power *and* will. (INCORRECT)

Exhausted *both in* power *and in* will. (CORRECT)

or

Exhausted in *both* power *and* will. (CORRECT)

53. LESS

The adjective *less* refers to quantity. If the reference is to number, then *fewer* must be used, e.g.

less bread, *but fewer* muffins

less traffic, but *fewer* cars

less power, but *fewer* powers

Note the following example:

There were *fewer people* there than usual.

54. IN ORDER THAT

In order that introduces an adverb-clause of purpose and should, therefore, be followed by a verb-form containing *may* or *might*.

The men worked extremely hard *in order that* the contract *could* be completed by the promised date.

Change 'could' to 'might'.

The firm have recently made special arrangements *in order that* all the employees *will be able to* acquire shares in the company.

Change 'will be able to' to 'may'.

55. THE SUBJUNCTIVE

In current usage the subjunctive mood is employed infrequently. However, there are circumstances in which it must on no account be replaced by the indicative. The following sentences are incorrect:

If I was you, I should not go.

Change 'was' to 'were'.

If he was here now, we would have a great time of it.

Change 'was' to 'were'.

I wish it *was* over.

Change 'was' to 'were'.

Punctuation

In order to assist the easy reading of a written sentence, certain stops or marks of punctuation are inserted to indicate where pauses would naturally be made in reading sentences aloud.

In current practice there is no rigid system of punctuation universally used, although certain rules are generally observed. However, on minor points practice varies with different writers, and special considerations sometimes lead a writer to depart deliberately from the conventional method of punctuation.

The rules given below are statements of the more commonly accepted practices of punctuation.

56. THE FULL STOP (.)

This is used:
(a) At the end of all sentences except direct questions or exclamations.

(b) After initials or abbreviated words:
J. Bloggs Esq.
S. Cook B.A. Hons. (Oxon.)
Dr. Finlay M.D.

Technically the abbreviated names of organizations and countries should carry full stops, e.g. U.N., T.G.W.U., U.S.A. However, they are nowadays more often found without punctuation:
UN, TGWU, USA
S. Cook BA Hons (Oxon)
Dr Finlay MD

(c) The full stop signals the end of a completed sentence. It therefore cannot appear until the main finite verb has been written.

57. THE COMMA (,)

(a) The comma indicates a short pause. It is used in sentences that contain a series of words belonging to the same part of speech, and forming a double or multiple subject, predicate or object, e.g.
Buses, cars, taxis and a whole host of cycle couriers were blocking the road through the City. (multiple subject)
Pavarotti entered stage left, advanced to the footlights, and began the opera's most popular aria. (multiple predicate)
From the plane we could see the long runway, the busy airport and massive sprawl of Prague, leading back into the country. (multiple object)

(b) A comma is used in sentences containing two or more phrases qualifying the same word:
Steffi's exemplary behaviour was good for tennis, her fellow competitors and for all Germans.
Freight can be sent by road, rail, sea or air.

(c) Commas mark off nouns used in address:
I think, Constable, you are mistaken.
Look here, son, get that work done.

(d) A comma will indicate a word or phrase in apposition:
Edinburgh, capital of Scotland, has a large community of drug addicts.

(e) Use a comma to separate words or phrases in a list:
Captain of Manchester United, captain of England, Captain Marvel!

(f) Participle phrases, when not used restrictively, employ a comma:
Having finished my business, I went home.
Note the restrictive use in the following sentence:
The effect produced by the news was immediate.

(g) A comma marks off an absolute construction:
Our car being now mended, we pressed on.

(h) Use a comma to mark off words and phrases like however, indeed, therefore, too, for instance, no doubt, in fact, of course:
This proved, however, to be an erroneous view.
Chandra and Kate were fluent in three languages, and Julian was, in fact, not so skilled.
Others saw, too, that the task would be beyond his powers.
I decided, therefore, to give his job to the women.
I realized, of course, that he was displeased.

(i) In direct speech, commas are used where a break is made in the speech in order to indicate who is speaking:
'But, listen to me,' protested Jamie, 'I can't afford a car-phone.'
Of course, if the break comes at the end of a spoken sentence, the insertion should be followed by a full stop:
'Rachel arrives tomorrow,' he replied. 'I shall meet her at the station.'

(j) In complex sentences, use a comma to separate an adverb-clause from a following main-clause:
If you think nothing more can be done, I am satisfied.
Although so many people are of your opinion, I am still unconvinced.
Note that single noun-clauses and restrictive adjective-clauses are not separated by a comma from the main statement.
I was of the opinion that he would be spotted in the city centre, and his sister would be discovered with him. (two noun clauses)
Billy was a man who impressed everyone he met, and who did much to help the others on the estate. (two restrictive adjective-clauses)

(k) In double sentences, use a comma to separate the two coordinate clauses when the second subject is expressed:
Martha now had overall control of the department, but she soon found that the cares of management were more than she could bear. (two coordinate clauses)
I asked what Mark was doing, and he answered that he was preparing for his computer class. (two coordinate clauses)
A comma is also used to separate two coordinate clauses, even though the second subject is not expressed, when the conjunction *but* is used to join the clauses:
I beat the knocker on the door, but received no answer.
A comma is also employed to separate a continuative relative-clause from its antecedent:
I went into the dusty study of the professor, who at once offered me sherry.

Note that restrictive relative-clauses are separated by a comma from the main statement (see (j) above).

(l) In multiple sentences, i.e. those containing three or more coordinate clauses, each of the main clauses is usually marked off by a comma:

The burly opponent sprang forward, but was not quick enough, and Carling managed to avoid the tackle.

She came into the lecture theatre, crossed to the desk, and sat down.

But this is not an invariable practice. As the following sentences show, the position of the comma can be altered to change the tempo of the sentence:

The burly opponent sprang forward, but Carling was too quick for him and avoided his tackle.

She came into the lecture theatre and crossed to the desk, where she sat down.

The last two examples serve to show that a rigid code of rules for punctuation *cannot* be formulated, and that some latitude must be left to language-users, who need to vary their punctuation according to the effect they wish to achieve.

58. COMMON ERRORS IN THE USE OF THE COMMA

There are three common errors in the use of the comma that should be guarded against.

(a) The use of a comma to separate a subject from its verb:

The Glasgow–Heathrow shuttle, came hurtling down the runway.

The comma after 'shuttle' is not needed, and its use is incorrect.

However, a long subject is sometimes followed by a comma in order to indicate that the subject has come to an end:

People who have never known the degradation of having no home and the humiliation of abject poverty, cannot understand what living on the streets is like.

This practice is unnecessary. A lucidly-written sentence would not need the comma. If a sentence is not clear without the comma it probably should be rewritten.

Double commas may, of course, be used between a subject and its verb to mark off a phrase or a clause:

Julie, who until then had remained silent, asked where they were to get the funding for a new business.

History, Henry Ford famously said, is bunk.

Spielberg's films, spectacular as they are, are not my favourites.

(b) The use of a comma to separate a verb from its object:

Turning to the judge, the defendant asked meekly, that he might be leniently treated.

Here, there is no need for a second comma after 'meekly', and so the punctuation can be dropped. However, in order to give special stress to 'meekly', it would be possible to insert commas before *and* after it.

Double commas can also be used between a verb and its object to mark off a clause or phrase, just as they may be used between a subject and its verb:

At last Paul saw, or so he thought, the first signs of life from the birds' nest.

(c) The use of the comma to separate a defining or restrictive relative clause from its antecedent:

The train, that can cross from London to Paris and then on to Berlin, is not yet in service.

The market donated food and blankets to those, who had suffered terribly during the earthquake.

In both these sentences the comma(s) should be omitted.

59. THE SEMICOLON (;)

The semicolon marks a longer pause than is indicated by a comma. It is not used to separate mere phrases or words, except in enumerations, and even in these its use with anything less weighty than a clause is somewhat clumsy.

It has four main uses.

(a) In double sentences to separate coordinate clauses when the conjunction is omitted:

To his superiors Simon showed a cringing humility; to his juniors he appeared as a petty tyrant.

(b) In double sentences to separate coordinate clauses when the conjunction is used, but when a longer pause is required than would be indicated by a comma:

The weather was stormy; but Damian pushed on, through snow and ice, until he reached Helvellyn's summit.

(c) A semicolon is also used when the coordinate clauses are long:

In the first place, it does not follow that those people who live on a diet of red meat will become stronger, healthier or more fit; and a comparison between conventional vegetarians, vegans and any other meat-eating people will often come out in favour of abstinence from meat.

The Japanese had at one time been interested in the plant, and bought the whole firm; and old Mr Thelwell took the money and retired to a cottage in Wales, where he kept chickens.

(d) Instead of a full stop, to separate a number of parallel statements forming a series grouped as one sentence:

Mike from the pub, who made himself Tom's legal guardian, continued to look after the lad and encourage him; local scouts and coaches from the big football clubs occasionally visited; he was often asked to trials; he was loyal throughout to the Rovers.

The primeval forests have disappeared; open-cast mines now scar the once densely-wooded landscape; villages of miners, men from the city, not from the forest, are dotted along the river's edge; the wildlife that made the Amazon famous is long gone; a railway stretches where the world's greatest forest once stood.

60. THE COLON (:)

The colon marks a longer pause than the semicolon or comma.

It has three principal uses.

(a) To separate two coordinate clauses when the second repeats, explains or simplifies the statement contained in the first:

Under their old bosses they had at least one resource: when the conditions became too bad, the work-force would walk out and call a strike.

Never feed the horse poor food: great energy and endurance are to be obtained only by the continued use of nutritious food.

If a person goes to university and idles away his or her time, there by and by follows a natural penalty: s/he is left to suffer the consequences of failing his or her exams.

(b) Before an enumeration:
Lyric poetry includes various types: the ode, the elegy, the sonnet and the song.

(c) Sometimes to introduce a quotation or direct speech:
Thoughtful as he was, David would recall Rousseau's words: 'Man is born free, but lives everywhere in chains.'
Putting his daughter on the train, Billy embraced her: 'Look after yourself, and you know where we are if you need us.'

61. INVERTED COMMAS (' ' or " ")

(a) Inverted commas, or speech marks, are used to indicate direct speech:
'Well done on your promotion, Steve,' he said to his brother.
'We'll have a couple more drinks,' he explained, 'and then we'll head off for the beach.'

(b) They are also used to indicate quotations from, or the titles of, novels, plays, television programmes, essays etc.
Shakespeare's 'Hamlet' or 'The Scottish Play' remains a popular choice with amateur dramatic societies and schools alike, though many of the more adventurous companies go for something trendy like Pinter's 'The Dumb Waiter', adaptations of 'Wuthering Heights', or just a good, modern comedy, like 'Having a Ball'. Even so, people are just as happy thumbing through a copy of the 'TV Times' and staying in to watch 'Coronation Street', so 'To be or not to be, That is the question . . .' loses out to 'Betty's hot pies in the Rover's Return'.
It is worth mentioning that in printed matter the titles of books, plays etc. are more commonly placed in italics, or, in the case of typescripts, underlined:
Nightmare on Elm Street III
The vibrant music in Peter Schaffer's *Amadeus* was of course Mozart's own *Concerto for Flute and Harp*.

62. THE DASH AND THE HYPHEN

(a) The dash (— or –) is used:

(i) To mark a parenthesis, or an abrupt change of thought:
In the end – to cut a long story short – Jack spilled the oysters all over the bar!
'Proceeding to the next item on the agenda – we'll have to work fast to get through this lot.'

(ii) Before a repeated word:
The indirect and more serious consequence is the effect on the town – a consequence that inevitably follows among people who are opposed to petty corruption in the town hall.
Hence the tendency to want to have more open forms of government for the people – a tendency which has sprung from positive needs, not just negative experiences – will become more prevalent.

(iii) It is also inserted before the demonstrative pronouns *these*, *those* and *such*, when they are used at the beginning of the main statement to sum up a

number of items previously mentioned:

> Less traffic on the roads, better public transport, less damage to the environment, cities where the roads are safe, and cleaner air – these will be the results of the green policies being discussed.

(b) The hyphen (-) is used:

(i) To form compound words:

sister-in-law
artist-in-residence
in-house photographer
booking-clerk

(ii) To divide words into syllables and at the end of a line:

Pa-ra-graph-, un-cer-tain

or to indicate a peculiar spoken form:

> The chants of Eng-er-land echoed around the city streets following the 'Big Match'.

63. THE INTERROGATION MARK AND THE NOTE OF EXCLAMATION

(a) The interrogation mark (?) is used after a direct question:

Has the day come?
Is it?

(b) The note of exclamation (!) is used after exclamatory words, phrases and sentences:

Jesus Christ!
Alas! he is gone.
How the mighty are fallen!

64. THE APOSTROPHE (')

(a) The apostrophe is used to indicate the omission of one or more letters:

Don't, e'er, o'er, it's

Note that *it's* is the contracted form of *it is*, whereas 'its' is the possessive pronoun.

(b) To denote the genitive case of nouns:

the girl's bike
the student's books
the students' union

65. THE OBLIQUE (/)

The oblique is used to signal alternatives in an elliptical style:

10/12, cars/trains, men/women, football/cricket

The oblique is not generally included in conventional lists of punctuation, but in recent years it has appeared more in printed literature by way of a compromise toward a non-sexist language. The *s/he* formation is increasingly common in English today.

> S/he will be expected to complete the following duties.

Spelling

66. THE ALPHABET

The sounds of spoken language are represented in writing by means of symbols known as the letters of the alphabet. In a perfect alphabet, every letter would represent one sound and one only, and each sound would have its own symbol. Judged by this standard, the English alphabet is obviously defective. We have not enough symbols to represent all the sounds, and hence:

(a) The same symbol may represent many different sounds, e.g.

a in rat, tall, many, mane, want, bare
o in hot, woman, whose, hero, son

(b) The same sound may be represented by various symbols, e.g.

hit, nymph, busy, women, sieve (All these words contain the vowel sound of hit.)
fate, champagne, pail, vein, they, reign, gauge, dahlia, steak (All these words contain the diphthongal sound of fate.)

On the other hand, some letters are superfluous, e.g.

q (qu might equally well be written kw), *x* (=ks or gs), *c* (=k or s).

In pointing out the deficiencies of the English alphabet, we are really calling attention to the fact that modern English spelling is not phonetic; i.e. it does not accurately and consistently represent the sounds of speech. The spelling of Old English was very nearly phonetic. How is it, then, that the spelling of today represents the spoken language so badly?

67. THE HISTORY OF ENGLISH SPELLING

The answer is, briefly, that modern spelling was fixed in the fifteenth century, and, so far as it represents any pronunciation at all, it represents the pronunciation of that century. Before that time the scribes had each spelt as he thought best, but when printing was invented and books began to multiply, it was found necessary to stick to some definite system. Thus the early printers produced a system of spelling which has persisted, with few changes, ever since. When it is added that English pronunciation has undergone many and far-reaching changes since Caxton's time, one reason for the lack of correspondence between the written word and the spoken sound will become clear. The symbol *gh* for instance, which is now silent in *sought*, *bought* etc., and which, in *laugh*, *enough* etc., has the sound of 'f', originally represented one and the same sound in all these words. Again, the symbols *ee* in *seed* or *ei* in *receive* in the fifteenth century represented a different sound from that of *ea* in *bead*, though these three symbols now all represent the same sound.

A further reason for the chaotic state of modern English spelling is to be found in the fact that even as early as the fifteenth century there were many irregularities, due largely to French scribes who had introduced symbols from their own language to represent English sounds. This explains the use of *c* for *s* in *city*, *mice* etc., *gu* for *g* in *guest*, *guess* etc., *qu* for OE *cw* in *quick*, *queen* etc., and *ou* or *ow* for the diphthongal sound in *house*, *cow* etc.

Further confusion resulted from attempts to make the spelling of certain words indicate their etymology. The Norman-French words *dette* and *doute*, for example, kept this spelling when they were first introduced into English. They were later written *debt* and *doubt* in order to show their connection with the Latin *debitum* and *dubitum*. The *b* has never been pronounced.

The spelling of English has many anomalies, but in spite of this there are certain rules that are useful to learn, because they have a wide and general application. English has assimilated a great number of words with classical derivation, and even a slight knowledge of the principles of their spelling will be of great use in deciding upon the correct English spelling. The use of double consonants offers many pitfalls to language users, but here also definite rules are generally followed, and a knowledge of them does much to lessen the terrors of English spelling. Besides these two main groups, there are many other instances where general principles can be profitably applied; however, as the exceptions would often prove as numerous as the examples, we have not given an exhaustive list, but only those rules which are clear and obvious.

68. A SUMMARY OF PRINCIPAL RULES

(a) Words and phrases of classical origin are familiar to modern English speakers and widely used; yet their written form often causes confusion, especially in respect of pairs of suffixes, such as *-able, -ible; -ative, -itive; -ation, -ition; -acious, -icious.*

English teachers used to cite the relevant rule from Latin grammar: nouns of the first declension and verbs of the first conjugation form their respective adjectives or nouns in *-a-*, while all others take the form with *-i-*. Today's teachers, however, cannot afford such confidence that everyone has enjoyed a classical education. The best advice, therefore, that can be offered to modern language users is to examine individual examples in order to know the proper spelling. The following words are among the most frequently misspelt:

indispensable	predicative
responsible	definitive
comparative	avaricious
nominative	voracious
accusative	

(b) Another pair of suffixes that are often confused is *-ent, -ant.*

Old school grammarians would have advised that *-ant* derives either from the present participle of first conjugation verbs in Latin, or from the French present participle. But for many modern students of orthography it has taken the launch of a national newspaper to resolve once and for all the correct spelling of independent!

Words that are frequently misspelt in this category are:

adherent	conversant
cogent	dependant (noun)
contingent	dominant
dependent (adj.)	flagrant
imminent	relevant
impudent	resonant
insolent	

(c) The prefixes *in-* and *e-* must be given careful attention.

When followed by *r* or *l*, the prefix *in-* becomes *ir-, il-*, thus doubling the consonant-letter. *E-* remains unchanged in all circumstances. This causes much confusion,

especially with pairs of words of which one has the prefix *e-* and the other *in-*.
The following are among the most commonly misspelt:

emigrate	illude
immigrate	erect
eminent	irradiate
imminent	elicit (verb)
elude	illicit (adj.)

(d) Before *b*, *m* or *p*, *in-* becomes *im-*, as with *imbue*, *immobile*, *impudent*. Before the other letters of the alphabet, *in-* remains unchanged: *indict*, *insidious*.

(e) As with *in-* above, some other prefixes are assimilated to certain consonant-letters: *ad-*, *con-*, *dis-*, *sub-*.

accessory (ad-)	diffident (dis-)
alleviate (ad-)	success (sub-)
aggravate (ad-)	suffix (sub-)
attract (ad-)	suggest (sub-)
collaborate (con-)	suppose (sub-)
commerce (con-)	resurrection (re-, sub-)
correct (con-)	

(f) In such words as acknowledge, acquaint, acquiesce, the assimilation of *ad-* is complete: both *k* and *q* following *ad-* always have this effect on *ad-*.

An understanding of these rules should help in the spelling of many groups of words that are often confused: exceed (*ex-*), succeed (*sub-*); illegible, ineligible.

(g) The use of double consonants

(i) One use of double consonants has been discussed in connection with the assimilation of consonants in certain Latin prefixes.

In words ending in a single consonant preceded by a single vowel and accented on the final syllable, the final consonant is doubled when a syllable is added:

begin, beginning
refer, referred
occur, occurred
But appeal, appealing

(ii) In similar words that are not accented on the final syllable, the final consonant is *not* doubled:

bigot, bigoted
develop, developed
benefit, benefited
But worship, worshipped; kidnap, kidnapped
The exceptions to this rule are words ending in *-l*:
quarrel, quarrelled
marvel, marvellous
jewel, jewellery

(iii) *All, full, fill, well* drop one *l* when used as the first or last syllables in compound words:

almighty
withal

awful
spoonful
fulfil
welcome

Note that, despite common usage to the contrary, *all right* is two words and not one (*alright* is incorrect).

(iv) Besides those covered by the foregoing rules, there are many words in which double consonants are used incorrectly instead of single ones, and vice versa:

absolute, adapt, adept, arrogant, conurbation, desiccate, disappear, disappoint, disaster, discriminate, estimate, inoculate, iridescent, militate, mitigate, peremptory, petulant, recommend, relative, parallel, occasionally (these single consonants are often wrongly doubled).

accessory, accommodation, apposite, collation, disappoint, vaccinate, vacillate (these double consonants are often wrongly written as single).

(h) Nouns and verbs formed from the same root often confuse language users. There are many such words in which the noun ends in -*ce* and the verb in -*se*:

practice, practise
advice, advise
council, counsel (although the last word is of course also a noun used in formal legal contexts)

(i) Abstract nouns formed from adjectives ending in -*ate*, or from nouns ending in -*at*, end in -*acy*:

accurate, accuracy
private, privacy
autocrat, autocracy
democrat, democracy

(j) Final -*y* preceded by a consonant changes to -*i*- in certain circumstances.

(i) Nouns whose singular ends in -*y* immediately following a consonant change the -*y* into the group -*ies* to form the plural:

lady, ladies
body, bodies
party, parties

Note that singulars in -*ey* merely add -*s* in the plural:

chimney, chimneys
valley, valleys
donkey, donkeys

(ii) Verbs that end in -*y* immediately following a consonant change -*y* into -*ied* to form the past tense or past participle:

embody, embodied
rally, rallied
But alloy, alloyed (where the -*y* is preceded by a vowel)

(k) Words ending in a single -*e* drop the -*e* when a syllable beginning with a vowel is added:

debate, debatable
excite, excitable
But excitement

(l) Where a word ends in -*ce* or -*ge*, and where the *c* or *g* is to remain soft, the -*e* is retained before -*able* and -*ous* in derivatives:

notice, noticeable
service, serviceable
trace, traceable
manage, manageable
advantage, advantageous
outrage, outrageous
But practice, practicable

(m) When a syllable rhymes with '*lee*' , *i* is put before *e*, except after *c*:

believe, retrieve, receive, receipt, siege
But seize, weird, weir

In such words as forfeit the 'ei' sound is shortened in pronunciation to 'i', as in 'bit'.

(n) Words ending in -*ence* and -*ense* often present difficulties to writers of English. There is *no* hard and fast rule to remember. The best guide may be to learn the following examples in -*ense*:

expense
license (verb, cf. noun *licence*)
tense
sense

(o) The use of -*ise* (-*isation*) and -*ize* (-*ization*) is largely, though not entirely, a matter of choice. Most words can be spelt with -*ise*; but not capsize, prize (reward; *but* prise, to lever), size. Some words cannot be spelt with -*ize*: franchise; excise, incise, etc.; exercise; compromise, surmise etc. (*but* itemize is acceptable); comprise, surprise etc.; advertise; improvise, revise, supervise etc. Whichever spelling is chosen should be used consistently.

A useful guide is whether an -*ise* verb makes an -*isation* noun; if it does, it can usually be spelt -*ize* (organize, organization; *but* improvise, improvisation)

-*yse*, not -*yze*: analyse, catalyse.

69. WORDS FREQUENTLY MISSPELT

Confusion is often caused by the similar pronunciation of the words concerned:

there (adverb of place), their (possessive adjective)
wear (verb), ware (noun), where (adverb of place)
whether (conjunction), weather (noun)
to (preposition), two (numeral adjective or pronoun), too (adverb)
here (adverb of place), hear (verb)
born (past participle), borne (past participle), bourne (noun)
four (numeral adjective or pronoun), for (preposition), forty (numeral adjective or pronoun), fore (noun or adjective), therefore (adverb)
tear (noun), tier (noun)
tear (verb and noun), tare (noun)
vale (noun), veil (noun and verb)
loose (adjective, or verb: to unfasten), lose (verb: to mislay)
choose (verb: present tense), chose (past tense)
not (negative adverb), knot (noun)

70. THE DIVISION OF WORDS IN WRITING

We are all acquainted with the practice of dividing words up into two when a whole word will not fit on to the end of a line on a page. Hyphenation of this sort is found in printed books, newspapers etc. However, modern desk-top publishing systems common to most offices are able to justify texts automatically, according to a user's wishes, thus avoiding the mechanical need to fit the words to the page.

For the purpose of handwriting, if one cannot write the whole word at the end of a line, there is no reason why one should not leave a space and carry the whole word over to the next line: and it is often better to do so. However, the division of words may be unavoidable when writing, and one should be careful to divide words correctly, so as to maintain the sense of the text. The following are useful guidelines:

(a) A word _must_ be divided into complete syllables. The division should come at the end of a syllable, never in the middle. Thus, monosyllables should never be divided, and such forms as tas/te, pha/se, with the last letters on a new line, must never be used.

(b) In order to divide words correctly it is necessary to know the constitution of syllables. As a general rule, words are divided grammatically: that is to say that the division comes after a prefix, or before a suffix.

The word 'relationship', for example, could be divided at any of these points:
re/la/tion/ship
'Accommodation' could be divided as follows:
ac/com/mo/da/tion
In these words it is to be noted that where there is a single consonant, the division should come before it; where there are two, the division comes between them.

(c) In words where one syllable ending in a vowel is followed by another syllable beginning with a vowel, division comes between the vowels. Examples of this are:
in/flu/ence
va/ri/ous
sci/en/tif/ic
pro/nun/ci/a/tion

(d) There are some suffixes, of Anglo-Saxon origin, that are put alone, regardless of the numbers of consonants preceding them. These are: -ing, -en, ed, -y.
danc/ing, mourn/ing, burst/ing
spok/en, weak/en, em/bold/en
worst/ed, test/ed, re/pre/sent/ed
mood/y, word/y

(e) It makes sense, of course, to recognize that -y divisions are not the same as -ly or -ty divisions, such as
god/ly, friend/ly
plen/ty, a/no/ny/mi/ty, per/spi/ca/ci/ty
This goes to show that the best rule is to decide according to sound rather than according to the etymology of the parts. Thus the root in loquacity is _loqu-_ but the division would never be loqu/acity, but lo/quacity.

Versification

71. RHYTHM

The sounds and rhythms that words throw up are an exciting dimension to language study. The rhythms of language can provide pieces of prose with a force to underline the measure and meaning of the sentences. A skilled writer can develop the euphonic qualities of his or her prose to help convey the meaning in a more or less strong fashion, according to his or her wishes.

But it is in verse, the language of poetry and song, that we find rhythm adapted to its limits. The accented and unaccented syllables of words can be arranged to form a pattern. We are often acquainted with rhythm-patterns in speech, even from our earliest days.

> Mary had a little lamb,
> Its fleece was white as snow.
> And everywhere that Mary went
> The lamb was sure to go.

Learning the simple songs of the nursery teaches us the uses of rhyme, such as the way the rhythm of a sentence places emphasis on certain words. It is, of course, easiest to recognize the regular rhythms of poetry, standing out against the blankness of normal speech. Consider the following sentences:

> Ít was my oríginal púrpose to táke a víew of the prínciples of the Nátional Assémbly with regárd to the gréat and fundaméntal estáblishments.

> His hóuse was knówn to áll the vágrant tráin: he chíd their wánderings, bút relíeved their páin. The lóng-remémbered béggar wás his guést, whose béard descénding swépt his áged bréast.

In these sentences the syllables that bear the accent or stress in reading have been marked. In the first sentence (which is prose) the accents are not arranged according to any special pattern. In the second (which is verse, though here printed as prose) the accents fall on alternate syllables, so that there is a regular rhythm.

Not all rhythm has to be a complex and lengthy construction. Any writer can use a rhythmic phrase to sharpen the focus of his or her sentence. Take another children's song for example:

> Pease pudding hot!
> Pease pudding cold!

This shows how rhythm has placed the contrasting options of hot and cold in stark opposition to each other, in the simple terms of a song. It is just another way of saying, 'You can have pease pudding either hot or cold,' but the versification (the way the sentences are divided up and measured against each other) has lent the sentence a simple rhythmic force appropriate for a child's song.

(a) When talking about verse it is important to realize that every word of more than one syllable has a natural stress on one of the syllables, for example prelíminary, unbóunded, prínciple. But it is easy to create rhythms with a sentence of words of one syllable, that is, monosyllabics.

> Jáck Sprát could éat no fát.
> His wífe could éat no léan.

(b) Much of the verse we are exposed to, whether it is in religious songs, chant or prayer, comic verse, or under the auspices of learning poetry in school, is recognizable by its distinct sentence construction. Many poets used to invert the position of words to create rhythmic sentences suitable for verse:

A mán he wás to áll the cóuntry déar. (VERSE)
He wás a mán déar to áll the cóuntry. (PROSE)

Other popular examples of this sort of sentence construction are:

Háil! the cónquering héro cómes.
Till déath us do párt.

(c) Rhyme, though an obvious feature of much verse, is not an essential feature. It is another means by which poets, composers etc. create a sense or mood in their writing, for example in

Oh, Marie's the *name*
Of his latest *flame*.

where the rhyme matches the up-tempo beat of an Elvis Presley song.

(d) Far from following the same pattern, patterns of rhythm can be changed to obtain a different poetic effect. Consider the following:

(i) Below, Auden's lines evoke the familiar rhythm of a steaming locomotive:

Thís is the Níght Mail cróssing the Bórder,
Brínging the chéque and the póstal órder.

(ii) Browning's verse is constructed to evoke the pace of the events described in the poem:

I spráng to the stírrup, and Jóris, and hé,
I gálloped, Dirck gálloped, we gálloped all thrée.

72. METRE

The various rhythms or metres are classified by dividing the lines up into units called feet. A metrical foot contains a stressed syllable, and usually one or more unstressed syllables.

Hence a line containing five stressed syllables (with no matter how many unstressed syllables) will contain five feet. Thus:

And fóols/who cáme/to scóff/remáined/to práy.
Take éach/man's céns/ure bút/resérve/thy júdgment.

Or here with four stressed syllables, and so four feet:

It cáme/upón/a míd/night cléar.

Metrical feet may be of different kinds according to the number of syllables they contain and the position of the stressed syllable. The various kinds of feet found in English verse have been given names taken from Latin and Greek versification. They are as follows.

Iambus

This consists of two syllables, an unstressed followed by a stressed one.

The wáy/was lóng,/the wínd/was cóld.

Trochee

The trochee also has two syllables, this time a stressed followed by an unstressed.

Ónce up/ón a/mídnight/dréary,
Whíle I/póndered/wéak and/wéary.

Anapaest

Three syllables, two unstressed followed by the stressed syllable.

From the cén/tre all roúnd/to the séa.

Dactyl

Three syllables with the stressed one coming first.

Táke her up/ténderly.

Amphibrach

Again three syllables, the stressed one between two unstressed ones.

There cáme to/the beách a/poor éxile/of Érin.

This line containing amphibrachs may also be regarded as consisting of anapaestic feet with an initial iambus:

There cáme/to the beách/a poor éx/ile of Érin.

The line then contains an extra unaccented syllable at the end. Such a line is said to be hypermetrical because it contains a mix of metres.

Free verse

It is important to realize that the above metrical systems are characteristics of stylized verse which have evolved through history. Contemporary poets may, of course, use or adapt such systems, but above all they have been noted for their use of free verse – a style which falls outside the rigorous traditional forms and is often difficult to distinguish from prose.

Here the modern poet, T.S. Eliot, begins his poem *The Waste Land* in such a style:

April is the cruellest month, breeding
Lilacs out of the dead land, mixing
Memory and desire, stirring
Dull roots with spring rain.

But he returns to a more rigorous rhythm elsewhere, with comic verse like

Macávitý's a mýstery cát,
He's cálled the hídden cláw.
For hé's the máster críminál
Who cán defý the láw.

73. SCANSION

To scan a line of verse is to divide it up into feet and to mark the stressed syllables so as to indicate the kind of metre.

In order to be comfortable reading or speaking verse the reader should be aware of the author's use of rhythm. A poet may or may not compose his or her verse to follow a rigid or definite pattern; such a pattern may vary throughout a piece. A poet will look to vary rhythms in order to suit the sense of the verse. Hence such variations as the following are found.

(1) The substitution of a stressed syllable for an unstressed syllable.

(2) The use of an unstressed or a half-stressed syllable where a fully stressed syllable should occur.

(3) The insertion of extra unaccented syllables.

(4) The omission of unaccented syllables.

These points are illustrated by examining the following passage from Shakespeare, where the normal line consists of five iambic feet – known as the iambic pentameter – but involves many variations.

> If mú/sic bé/the fóod/of lóve,/pláy ón;
> Gíve me/excéss/of ít,/that súr/feiting,
> The ápp/etíte/may síck/en, ánd/só díe.
> That stráin/agáin!/it hád/a dý/ing fáll:
> Ó! it/came ó'er/my eár/like the/swéet soúnd
> That bréathes/upón/a bánk/of ví/olets,
> Stéaling/and gív/ing ód/our! Enóugh!/no móre:

In lines 1, 3 and 5 the final foot contains two stressed syllables. Prosodists (those who study the science of versification) would refer to this foot as a *spondee*.

However, William Blake's poem 'Jerusalem', now a popular hymn, is an example of a rigorous structure in four-foot iambics:

> And díd/those féet/in án/cient tíme
> Walk úp/on Eńg/land's móun/tains gréen?
> And wás/the hó/ly Lámb/of Gód
> On Eńg/land's pléas/ant pás/tures séen?

The commonest measures in English verse are lines of four or five iambic feet, just like the lines from Blake above. Anapaestic four-foot verse is also fairly common. The following is an example of this:

> How pléa/sant to knów/Mr Léar!
> Who has wrít/ten such vól/umes of stúff!
> Some thínk/him ill tém/pered and quéer,
> But a féw/think him pléa/sant enóugh.

(Edward Lear)

Below is an example of iambic verse in alternate four-foot and three-foot lines; the three-foot lines are hypermetrical.

> Yea, déck/your lów/er límbs/in pánts,
> Yoúrs áre/the límbs,/my swéeting.
> You lóok/divíne/as yóu/advánce –
> Have you séen/yoursélf/retréating?

(Ogden Nash)

Note the extra syllable in the first foot of line 4, and the spondee in the first foot of line 2.

> As tráv/ellers óft/look báck/at éve
> When éast/ward dárk/ly góing,
> To gáze/upón /that líght/they léave
> Still fáint/behínd /them glówing,
> Só, when/the clóse/of pléa/sure's dáy
> To glóom/hath néar/consígned us,
> We túrn/to cátch/one fád/ing ráy
> Of jóy/that's léft/behínd us.

(Thomas Moore)

This again is iambic verse in alternate four-foot and three-foot lines. Lines 2, 4, 6 and 8 are hypermetrical. The first foot of line 5 is a trochee.

> Like the léaves/of the fór/est when súm/mer is gréen,
> That hóst/with their bánn/ers at sún/set were séen;
> Like the léaves/of the fór/est when áut/umn hath blówn,
> That hóst/ on the mór/row lay wíth/er'd and strówn.

(Lord Byron)

The above is anapaestic four-foot verse. The first foot of lines 2 and 4 is an iambus. The introduction of an occasional iambic foot is a characteristic feature of anapaestic verse. Sometimes two lines of three feet or four feet are combined and made into one long line:

> He had ón/ly a húnd/red séa/men // to wórk/the shíp/ and to fíght,
> And he sáiled/awáy/from Flór/es // till the Spán/iard cáme/ in síght,
> With his húge/ séa-cást/les héav/ing // upón/the wéath/er brów.

(Lord Tennyson)

Each of these lines might be divided into two three-foot lines.

74. CAESURA (CUTTING)

When a marked pause occurs in the middle of a line, it is known as a caesura. Such internal pauses are very prominent in longer lines that are really combinations of two short lines. However, caesurae are common in lines of five feet. There may be other minor pauses besides the main pause or caesura. The caesura frequently coincides with a punctuation mark. The caesura in the following lines is marked with //.

> Milton!//thou shouldst be living at this hour:
> England hath need of thee;//she is a fen
> Of stagnant waters://altar, sword, and pen,
> Fireside,//the heroic wealth of hall and bower,
> Have forfeited their ancient English dower
> Of inward happiness.//We are selfish men:
> Oh! raise us up,//return to us again;
> And give us manners, virtue, freedom, power.
>
> Thy soul was like a star,//and dwelt apart;
> Thou hadst a voice whose sound was like the sea,
> Pure as the naked heavens,//majestic, free,
> So didst thou travel on life's common way
> In cheerful godliness;//and yet thy heart
> The lowliest duties on herself did lay.

(William Wordsworth)

Notice that the caesurae are placed to vary the rhythm of the verse and to lend emphasis to the introduction of new ideas within the poem.

75. END-PAUSE

Metrical language is divided up into units, the unit being the line or 'verse'. In prosody the technical name for a line is a 'verse': a collection of 'verses' forms a 'stanza'. Thus at the end of each verse there is a pause; and in the writings of some poets this end-pause is regularly observed:

> Beside yon straggling fence that skirts the way,
> With blossomed furze unprofitably gay,

There, in his noisy mansion, skilled to rule,
The village master taught his little school;
A man severe he was, and stern to view,
I knew him well, as every truant knew.

(Oliver Goldsmith)

In the following passage, it will be seen that the sense is frequently carried over from one line to the next, so that there is no pause at the end of the verse:

Thus with the year
Seasons return, but not to me returns
Day, or the sweet approach of ev'n or morn,
Or sight of vernal bloom, or summer's rose,
Or flocks, or herds, or human face divine;
But cloud instead, and ever-during dark
Surrounds me, from the cheerful ways of men
Cut off, and for the book of knowledge fair,
Presented with a universal blank
Of nature's works, to me expung'd and ras'd,
And wisdom at one entrance quite shut out.

(John Milton)

Lines such as these, lacking an end-pause, are called 'run-on' lines.

76. RHYME, ASSONANCE, ALLITERATION

(a) Rhyme, a customary ornament of English verse, is the repetition of the same sound at the end of two or more lines. Rhymes of words of one syllable are called single or masculine:
hoard – board
bent – sent
Rhymes of two-syllable words are called double or feminine:
measures – pleasures
crying – drying
Treble rhymes also occur:
pattering – chattering
Rhyme is the feature of verse which is most easily identified. In the stanza below, Robert Service makes use of rhyme to construct his verse:

Then I ducked my head, and the lights went out, and two guns blazed in the
dark;
And a woman screamed, and the lights went up, and two men lay stiff and *stark*.
Pitched on his head, and pumped full of lead, was Dangerous Dan Mc*Grew*,
While the man from the creeks lay clutched to the breast of the lady that's known
as *Lou*.

Yet rhyme does not have to occur within the structure of a rigid rhyme scheme. The following is an example of how the rhyming qualities of words are exploited without the necessity for a rigid pattern:

Never *more*;
Miranda,
Never *more*.
Only the high peaks *hoar*:
And Aragon a torrent at the *door*.
No *sound*

In the *walls* of the *Halls* where *falls*
The *tread*
Of the feet of the *dead* to the *ground*.
No *sound*;
But the *boom*
Of the far Water*fall* like *Doom*.

(Hilaire Belloc)

Belloc's verse contains instances of internal rhyme where words in the same line rhyme, as with 'walls' and 'halls'.

(b) Assonance

Assonance is sometimes used instead of perfect rhyme. It occurs when two words contain the same or similar vowel sounds in conjunction with different consonantal sounds, as exemplified in the popular saying

A stitch in *time* saves *nine*.

where the effect of the vowel-sound in 'time' and 'nine' is the same, but where the consonants (here 'm' and 'n' in the respective words) differ, thus preventing it from being a pure rhyme as 'time'/'lime' or 'nine'/'Rhine' would be. Similar assonant effects occur in the lines from Tennyson and Squeeze below.

Half a league, half a league,
Half a league *onward*,
All in the valley of Death,
Rode the six *hundred*.

(Tennyson)

And so it's my *assumption*
I'm really up the *junction*.

(Squeeze)

(c) Alliteration

Words are said to alliterate when they begin with the same letter. In Anglo-Saxon verse, alliteration filled the place now occupied by rhyme. In modern verse, however, alliteration is an ornament used to link words or phrases, and it is valued for its euphonic qualities. Consider Gerard Manley Hopkins's alliterative style, recalling Anglo-Saxon poetic techniques, in describing 'The Windhover':

I caught this morning morning's minion, kingdom of daylight's dauphin, dapple-
    dawn-drawn Falcon, in his riding
Of the rolling level underneath him steady air, and striding
High there, how he rung upon the rein of a wimpling wing
In his ecstasy! then off, off forth on swing.

Alliteration can be deftly introduced to add effect to a single line, as with the popular song from Simon and Garfunkel:
    The *S*ound of *S*ilence.

77. BLANK VERSE

This is simply unrhymed verse and is commonly used, especially by dramatists. Most people are acquainted with blank verse through the work of Shakespeare, who wrote using a blank verse line which consisted of five iambic feet, the iambic pentameter.

78. STANZAS

Some of the most common stanzas or verse-groups used in English are listed below.

(a) Couplets

Pairs of lines that rhyme are called couplets. Couplets are not generally considered to be full stanzas, but it is convenient to deal with them here. Couplets are either made up of four-foot verses (sometimes called octosyllabic), or of five-foot verses (sometimes called decasyllabic). Five-foot iambic lines rhyming in pairs are called heroic couplets (because they were regarded as the metre appropriate to 'heroic' or epic poetry in classical literature).

> So keep the scarlet standard *high*,
> Beneath its folds we'll live and *die*;
> Though cowards flinch and traitors *sneer*,
> We'll keep the red flag flying *here*.

The political anthem, the 'Red Flag', is an example of the octosyllabic couplet.

> O'er the pale marbles shall they join their *heads*,
> And drink the falling tears each other *sheds*;
> Then sadly say, with mutual pity *mov'd*,
> 'Oh may we never love as these have *lov'd*.'

Here, Alexander Pope adopts the form of the heroic couplet.

In the example below Shelley constructs a pair of couplets in a stanza of three trochaic feet with an extra syllable at the end of the line. Line 2 varies the metre: it is made up of four iambs.

> I met Murder on the *way*–
> He had a mask like Castle*reagh*–
> Very smooth he looked, yet *grim*;
> Seven blood-hounds followed *him*:

Some writers of heroic couplets can avoid the end-pause and carry over the sense from one line and one couplet to another. For this feature the French term *enjambement* is used.

> O that those lips had language! Life has passed
> With me but roughly since I heard thee last.
> Those lips are thine – thy own sweet smiles I *see*,
> The same that oft in childhood solaced *me*;
> Voice only fails, else how distinct they *say*,
> 'Grieve not, my child, chase all thy fears *away*!'
> The meek intelligence of those dear *eyes*
> (Blest be the art that can immortal*ize*,
> The art that baffles Time's tyrannic *claim*
> To quench it!) here shines on me still the *same*.

> *(William Cowper)*

(b) Four-line stanzas

The four-line stanza, or quatrain, is the commonest English stanza. The following are the chief varieties.

(i) Long metre

Four four-foot iambic lines, rhyming *a b a b* thus:

> I wander thro' each chartered street,   a
> Near where the charter'd Thames does flow,   b

And mark in every face I meet	a
Marks of weakness, marks of woe.	b

(William Blake)

(ii) Common metre
Alternate four-foot and three-foot lines, rhyming *a b a b*:

For when the morn came dim and sad	a
And chill with early showers,	b
Her quiet eyelids closed – she had	a
Another morn than ours.	b

(Thomas Hood)

Most of the old ballads were written in common metre, though in them the first and third lines generally do not rhyme. The scansion of ballad-poetry has a peculiar feature: the number of unstressed syllables in the line is not fixed, although the lines regularly have alternately four and three stressed syllables. A good example of this principle of scansion occurs in Coleridge's *The Ancient Mariner*.

(iii) The heroic quatrain or elegiac stanza
Four five-foot iambic lines, rhyming *a b a b*:

The curfew tolls the knell of parting day,	a
The lowing herd wind slowly o'er the lea,	b
The ploughman homeward plods his weary way,	a
And leaves the world to darkness and to me.	b

(Thomas Gray)

(iv) Anapaestic four-line stanza
Four-foot lines, rhyming *a a b b*:

The Assyrian came down like a wolf on the fold,	a
And his cohorts were gleaming in purple and gold;	a
And the sheen of their spears was like stars on the sea,	b
When the blue wave rolls nightly on deep Galilee.	b

(Lord Byron)

(c) Seven-line stanza: 'rhyme royal'
Seven five-foot iambic lines, rhyming *a b a b b c c*:

Hawthorne had lost his motley livery;	a
The naked twigs were shivering all for cold	b
And, dripping down the tears abundantly,	a
Each thing (methought) with weeping eye me told	b
The cruel season, bidding me withhold	b
Myself within; for I was gotten out	c
Into the fields whereas I walked about.	c

(Thomas Sackville)

(d) Eight-line stanza: 'ottava rima'
Eight five-foot iambic lines, rhyming *a b a b a b c c*. Used by Keats in *Isabella*, and by Byron in *Don Juan* and *The Vision of Judgment*.

The angels all were singing out of tune,	a
And hoarse with having little else to do,	b
Excepting to wind up the sun and moon,	a
Or curb a runaway young star or two,	b
Or wild colt of a comet, which too soon	a
Broke out of bounds o'er th'ethereal blue,	b

Splitting some planet with its playful tail,   c
As boats are sometimes by a wanton whale.   c

(Lord Byron)

(e) Nine-line 'Spenserian stanza'

Eight five-foot iambic lines, followed by a six-foot iambic line called an
'Alexandrine'. Rhyme-scheme: *a b a b b c b c c*. The first eight lines are really a
combination of two heroic quatrains connected by a common rhyme.

This stanza was developed by the Elizabethan poet Edmund Spenser, who used
it in his massive work, *The Faerie Queene*. It has since been used by poets wishing
to evoke a sense of archaism, notably Shelley in *Adonais*, Keats in *The Eve of Saint
Agnes*, and Byron in *Childe Harold*.

Roll on, thou deep and dark-blue Ocean – roll!   a
Ten thousand fleets sweep over thee in vain;   b
Man marks the earth with ruin – his control   a
Stops with the shore; upon the watery plain   b
The wrecks are all thy deed, nor doth remain   b
A shadow of man's ravage, save his own,   c
When for a moment, like a drop of rain,   b
He sinks into the depths with bubbling groan –   c
Without a grave, unknell'd, uncoffin'd, and unknown.   c

(Lord Byron)

(f) The sonnet

The sonnet is a verse-form of fourteen five-foot iambic lines used for a complete
poem. It was developed in Italy and introduced to this country in the sixteenth
century. The sonnet was a favourite form with the Elizabethans, and Shakespeare,
Spenser, Sidney, Sir Thomas Wyatt and the Earl of Surrey all wrote famous sonnet
collections. In the seventeenth century Milton used the form, but in the following
century it fell out of use. The Romantic poets Wordsworth, Keats and others
revived the sonnet as a poetic form and many poets still use it.

We can roughly divide the sonnet into two types.

(i) Petrarchan

Sonnets of the Petrarchan type follow the model set by the Italian lyric poet
Petrarch (1304–74). They consist of two parts – the octave (first eight lines) and the
sestet (last six lines). The octave is composed of two quatrains, the rhyme-scheme
being *a b b a a b b a*; the sestet has two or three new rhymes arranged variously. In
the strict Petrarchan sonnet there should be a break in the sense at the end of the
octave, so that a new turn of thought is introduced by the sestet.

Much have I travell'd in the realms of gold,
And many goodly states and kingdoms seen;
Round many western islands have I been
Which bards in fealty to Apollo hold.
Oft of one wide expanse had I been told
That deep-brow'd Homer ruled as his demesne:
Yet did I never breathe its pure serene
Till I heard Chapman speak out loud and bold:
– Then felt I like some watcher of the skies
When a new planet swims into his ken;
Or like stout Cortez, when with eagle eyes
He stared at the Pacific – and all his men
Look'd at each other with a wild surmise –
Silent, upon a peak in Darien.

(Keats: On First Looking into Chapman's Homer)

(ii) Shakespearian

The sonnets of William Shakespeare (1564–1616) consist of three quatrains with alternate rhymes, followed by a rhyming couplet. The complete rhyme-scheme is *a b a b c d c d e f e f g g*. In the Shakespearian sonnet the thought is carried right through until it reaches a climax in the final couplet.

> When in disgrace with fortune and men's eyes
> I all alone beweep my outcast state,
> And trouble deaf heaven with my bootless cries,
> And look upon myself, and curse my fate,
> Wishing me like to one more rich in hope,
> Featured like him, like him with friends possest,
> Desiring this man's art, and that man's scope,
> With what I most enjoy contented least;
> Yet in these thoughts myself almost despising,
> Haply I think on thee – and then my state,
> Like to the lark at break of day arising
> From sullen earth, sings hymns at heaven's gate;
> For thy sweet love remember'd such wealth brings
> That then I scorn to change my state with kings.

(Shakespeare: Sonnet xxix)

Part Two: Vocabulary

Diction

By the term 'diction' is meant the choice and arrangement of words. It may at first seem that anyone who can speak the English language correctly and fluently should find little difficulty in the choice and arrangement of words when writing. But such a supposition ignores the fact that the written language is not the same as the spoken language. Written English is an artificial language, more formal and exact than spoken English; it is the product of generations of men and women of letters who have established a definite tradition in the matter of form and expression. This is not to say that all great writers have adopted the same style. But the 'classic' writers have set certain standards in literary expression to which all who wish to write well would be advised to pay heed. Such writers have in fact become classic because they succeeded in enshrining in literature the permanent element of the spoken language of their day (and the spoken language is undergoing continual change from one generation to another), so that their written language was not for their own age only but for all time.

The succeeding sections of this chapter contain advice on how best to avoid the most common pitfalls of style when writing formal English.

79. THE CHOICE OF WORDS

(a) Colloquialisms and slang
Colloquial expressions used in familiar conversation are often regarded by grammarians as 'incorrect' English, that is, unsuitable for formal literary contexts, such as letter-writing. Slang words may often be identified exclusively with the dialect of a particular social or ethnic group. Such language may be fashionable for a time but subsequently lose popularity. Because of their ephemerality colloquialisms such as 'cool', 'wicked', 'hype' (a slang abbreviation of 'hyperbole') tend to date written language and are, therefore, best avoided in formal writing.

It should be noted that dialect is not ephemeral and can be used as an integral part of literary style when it is appropriate to the subject-matter, for example in Alice Walker's novel *The Color Purple*.

(b) Archaic words
Methinks, perchance, yonder, ere, whereof, all belong to the diction of a previous age and are, thus, out of place in modern speech or prose. However, such archaisms can be used intentionally to convey a sense of history or high-mindedness (especially in poetry), or perhaps as weapons of irony or humour.

(c) Clichés (or hackneyed phrases)
Certain expressions which were undoubtedly striking when first employed have lost all their original power of suggestion through over-use: e.g. last but not least, the fair sex, slowly but surely, conspicuous by its absence.

(d) Redundancy of expression
The use of unnecessary words takes various forms.

(i) Tautology.

This occurs when the same thing is said twice in different words:

They came one after the other in succession.

Here the phrase 'in succession' is synonymous with 'one after the other'. Similarly, tautology occurs in

Gradually, little by little, we forced our way through the obstacles.

(ii) Pleonasm.

A word is pleonastic when its meaning is implied in that of some other word in the sentence.

To see the snow-capped mountains far away is one of the most glorious sights.

The speed of the car was too fast.

We returned back home.

The reason why he did not come was because he was ill.

The pleonastic use of 'as to' is very common.

I began thinking as to what to say if my opinion were asked.

(iii) Verbosity.

A sentence is verbose when many words are used to express what could be said equally well in a few.

In my opinion the remuneration received by the subordinate officials in this office exceeds by a very considerable amount what is generally paid by other similar firms.

This could be expressed more simply (and, therefore, more effectively).

I think the junior staff in this office get far higher pay than they would elsewhere.

A prevalent form of verbosity is the 'officialese' found in Government documents, ministerial pronouncements or in the statements issued by public bodies, business organizations, trade unions and the like.

It is our considered opinion that the feeling of dissatisfaction is likely to assume considerable proportions in the immediate future.

Evidently, the same idea could be expressed more concisely (and much less pompously) thus:

We think that unrest will soon become widespread.

(iv) Periphrasis (or circumlocution).

This means a roundabout way of saying a simple thing which usually results in verbosity. For example, third-rate writers like to refer to Shakespeare as 'the bard of Avon', or to Nelson as 'the hero of Trafalgar'. Periphrasis is often used to avoid the undesirable repetition of a name. However, undue repetition can best be avoided by constructing a sentence so that pronouns may be effectively employed.

The fans were hoping that A and B would play in the match against Italy but the Spurs goalkeeper has pulled a hamstring and the Liverpool striker has been dropped by the manager.

Here 'the Spurs goalkeeper' means simply 'A', and 'the Liverpool striker' means 'B'.

Circumlocution may often be used as a euphemism or with intent at irony or humour.

It cannot be denied that the archbishop's most serious frailty was his habit of partaking too freely of alcoholic stimulants.

80. THE ARRANGEMENT OF WORDS

(a) Rule of proximity

All qualifying words, phrases and clauses should be placed as near as possible to the words to which they refer. If this rule is not observed, ambiguity will arise.

(i) Qualifying word:
This lift must only be used by the staff. (INCORRECT)
This lift must be used by the staff only. (CORRECT)

(ii) Qualifying phrase:
Car for sale by original owner with full MOT. (INCORRECT)
Car with full MOT for sale by original owner. (CORRECT)

(iii) Qualifying clause:
I do not recommend you to buy this house because the train service is so poor. (INCORRECT)
Because the train service is so poor, I recommend you not to buy this house. (CORRECT)

Particular attention should be taken in placing the correlatives *either . . . or, neither . . . nor, not only . . . but also, rather than . . .* etc.

She was not only fond of books but also of music. (INCORRECT)
She was fond not only of books but also of music. (CORRECT)

(b) Ambiguity
Obscurity in meaning can result from ambiguous phrasing.

(i) The vague use of pronouns occurs particularly in reported speech.
The counsel asked the witness whether he might take it for granted that what he had just said represented all he knew about the matter.

Here it is not clear whether the second 'he' refers to 'counsel' or to 'witness'.

(ii) The omission of necessary words can lead to misunderstanding.
The new ministers distrusted the American Ambassador, as much as their predecessors.

Insert 'had' after 'predecessors'.

The qualifications for a teacher and lecturer are not the same.

Insert 'a' before 'lecturer' to show that two distinct persons are referred to.

(c) Euphony
Prose, no less than verse, should aim to please the ear when read aloud. Euphony results from a harmonious combination of words with respect to sonority and rhythm. Some of the principal faults in diction which lead to the violation of euphony are given below with examples.

(i) Prepositions.
A passage will read awkwardly if it contains too many prepositions.

The secretary was asked to record a minute of the appreciation of the committee of the work done by the special sub-committee in connection with this matter.

(ii) Rhyme.
An unintentional rhyme can distract attention and disrupt the balance of a sentence.

Leisure is an inestimable treasure to those who make proper use of it.

A similar problem arises from the inharmonious conjunction of similar sounds.

He intends to pursue a course of intensive study.

I thought he expressed excessive diffidence with regard to the success of the project.

Limitation of armaments is required if more peaceful relations are to be established between the nations of the Middle East.

(iii) Relative pronouns.

Care must be taken not to introduce a sequence of clauses that do not all refer to the same antecedent.

These are the politicians who are fiercest in their denunciation of those who are attacking this evil, which is so widespread.

He has written a book which contains a chapter which blasphemes against the Sacred Prophet.

Figures of speech

In speaking and in writing we frequently depart from simple, direct or factual forms of statement and use figures of speech in order to heighten the effect. Often figures of speech may be strictly ungrammatical, but they are acceptable if used intentionally for a particular literary purpose.

81. SIMILE AND METAPHOR

Both simile and metaphor are figures which make use of comparison. They are figurative comparisons in that they compare things which are essentially different but which have some point of similarity. For example, to compare an ocean liner to a rowing-boat is unfigurative in that they are both essentially the same: they are both floating vessels. However, a ship and a camel are essentially different, yet when we use the metaphor 'the camel is the ship of the desert', we are aware of some features which the camel and the ship share.

(a) Simile
A simile is the definite statement of similarity between two different things which have some features in common. Similes are generally introduced by 'like' or 'as':

The saw cut through the wood like a knife through butter.

Or in a more literary form:

Let us go then, you and I,
When the evening is spread out against the sky
Like a patient etherized upon a table.

(T.S. Eliot)

(b) Metaphor
This is the implied resemblance of things which are ostensibly very different. Metaphor is implied since it does not make use of 'like' or 'as':

A stream of abuse flowed from his mouth.

An example of a metaphor taken from literature:

the boa-constrictor's coil
Is a fossil.

(Ted Hughes)

(c) Mixed metaphor
Weakness in writing sometimes occurs through the bringing together of two incongruous comparisons in one sentence. This is called mixed metaphor. It weakens the effect of the individual metaphor by attempting to sustain the figure through a new and unrelated figure. This is clear in

This world with all its trials is the furnace through which the soul must pass before it is ripe for the next world.

The metaphor of burning is not congruous with the metaphor of ripening.

82. ALLEGORY

An allegory has been defined as an extended metaphor. An initial metaphor is sustained throughout a whole narrative, for example George Orwell's *Animal Farm*. The actions of the animals imply human behaviour and this figure is carried through the whole of the novel. The reader is intended to see the resemblance between the facts of the story and the ideas which lie beneath. Fables and parables are short allegories.

83. PERSONIFICATION

Inanimate objects or abstract ideas are written or spoken of as if they were alive and had a personality of their own.

Imagine this midnight moment's forest:
Something else is alive
Beside the clock's loneliness.

(Ted Hughes)

Personification is a form of metaphor since it works upon an implied similarity between a feature of the inanimate object and its human counterpart.

84. ANTITHESIS ('SETTING AGAINST')

In this figure effective contrast is obtained by balancing one word or idea against another:

Prosperity doth best discover vice, but adversity doth best discover virtue.

(Francis Bacon)

True wit is nature to advantage drest,
What oft was thought, but ne'er so well exprest.

(Alexander Pope)

85. PARADOX

A statement which appears to contradict itself, often made intentionally to emphasize a point.

The child is father of the man.

(William Wordsworth)

Stone walls do not a prison make,
Nor iron bars a cage.

(Richard Lovelace)

86. OXYMORON

A compressed form of paradox in which two apparently contradictory words are brought together to form a new word and idea, e.g. bitter-sweet, love-hate.

87. EPIGRAM

In literature the term epigram is used to denote a short poem ending in a witty or satirical turn of thought.

Here lies our sovereign lord the king,
Whose promise none relies on;
He never said a foolish thing,
Nor ever did a wise one.

(Earl of Rochester)

The figure of speech known as epigram consists of a brief pointed saying, generally expressed antithetically or involving an apparent contradiction.

Every man desires to live long; but no man would be old.

(Jonathan Swift)

Vision is the art of seeing things invisible.

(Jonathan Swift)

88. APHORISM

A short proverbial saying which briefly conveys an idea or truth.

A proverb is one man's wit and all men's wisdom.

(Lord John Russell)

89. CLIMAX

In this figure a cumulative effect is created. The main point of the sentence is led up to by degrees. The writer begins with the least important idea and ends with the most important.

Some books are to be tasted, others to be swallowed, and some few to be chewed and digested.

(Francis Bacon)

90. ANTICLIMAX OR BATHOS

The opposite of climax. The ideas or things listed increase in importance until the last, which is the least important. This figure is sometimes deliberately used for humorous effect.

Not louder shrieks to pitying heaven are cast,
When husbands or when lapdogs breathe their last.

(Alexander Pope)

Here thou, great Anna, whom three realms obey,
Dost sometimes counsel take – and sometimes tea.

(Alexander Pope)

91. ELLIPSIS

The omission of a word or words from a sentence in order to compress the meaning.

While (I was) crossing the road, I looked both ways.

92. METONYMY ('CHANGE OF PLACES')

The use of a word or phrase to replace or imply another to which it is in some way related. It is a form of metaphor, but is not a true metaphor in that it works on a definite relationship between the two elements rather than any similarity. For example, the pen (the power of literature) is mightier than the sword (physical force). Also:
On the death of his brother he succeeded to the throne (being king).
The House of Commons (the members of the House) returns from its summer recess today.
I was reading Shakespeare (the plays of Shakespeare).

93. SYNECDOCHE

This figure, which is similar to metonymy, is based upon the relation of parts to the whole. A part or element of something is used to represent the whole, for instance when we speak of a king or queen as the crown. The following are examples of common usage:

(a) The small represents the whole:
All hands (the crew members) on deck!

(b) The material represents the object:
Sonorous metal (trumpets) blowing martial sound.

(John Milton)

(c) An individual represents a group:
Some mute inglorious Milton here may rest,
Some Cromwell guiltless of his country's blood.

(Thomas Gray)

(d) The abstract represents the tangible:
All the ability of the Football League is present in this team.

94. HYPERBOLE

A figure of speech consisting of exaggerated statement, which is used for effect, and intended to express strong feeling rather than to be taken literally.
                    Not in the legions
Of horrid hell can come a devil more damn'd
In evils to top Macbeth.

(William Shakespeare)

95. INNUENDO

An indirect comment where something is hinted at or implied without being stated outright. Innuendos are often used in the context of coarse comedy, for example, in the language of popular journalism.
The *Sport* gets Britain up in the morning.

96. EUPHEMISM

Euphemism is the use of a mild, indirect or pleasant expression to replace one that is considered too harsh or likely to offend. For example, dying can be spoken of as: to pass away, to go to a better world, to pass over. Euphemism is a form of synonym (see p.80).

97. LITOTES

Litotes is an intentional understatement. The writer affirms something by denying its opposite:
I am a citizen of no mean city (I am a citizen of a great city).
He is no fool (he is very intelligent).

98. ONOMATOPOEIA (ECHOISM)

This figure occurs when the sound of words suggests the sense, e.g. splash, bang, buzz. Some literary examples are:

Blow, winds, and crack your cheeks!

(William Shakespeare)

By the bang of blood in the brain deaf the ear.

(Ted Hughes)

99. APOSTROPHE

This figure describes a piece of writing in which the writer addresses an absent thing or person as if he, she or it were able to answer.

Ethereal minstrel! Pilgrim of the sky!
Dost thou despise the earth where cares abound?

(William Wordsworth)

Milton! thou shouldst be living at this hour.

(William Wordsworth)

100. PUN

A pun is a homonym. It is the use of a word in order to suggest two or three different meanings, or the use of two or more words of the same or nearly the same sound. Puns are usually used for a humorous effect, e.g.

When I am dead, I hope it may be said:
'His sins were scarlet, but his books were read.'

(Hilaire Belloc)

There is a pun on read (the verb) and red (the colour) which are homonyms in that they have the same sound but different meanings.

101. IRONY

Irony is a style or tone of writing as much as it is a figure of speech. Irony is the use of words in which the intended meaning is the opposite of what is actually said, but which allows the writer's true meaning to be perceived by the reader. The writer's (or speaker's) true meaning can usually be deduced from the context in which the figure appears. For example, in Shakespeare's *Julius Caesar*, Mark Antony's use of the address 'honourable men' is ironic since it is clear from the context of this speech that he does not consider them to be honourable. In the following passage from Dickens, the writer describes the Old Bailey as it was in 1780.

It was famous for the pillory, *a wise old institution*, that inflicted a punishment of which no one could foresee the extent; also for the whipping post, *another dear old institution*, *very humanizing and softening to behold in action*; also for extensive transactions in blood money, *another fragment of ancestral wisdom*, systematically leading to the most frightful mercenary crimes that could be committed under heaven.

The italicized phrases, whilst superficially approbatory, are in fact ironic, as can be deduced from their context in a passage which is a condemnation of punitive excess.

Often whole works are ironic, for example *A Modest Proposal* by Jonathan

Swift, in which the writer ostensibly proposes that children should be eaten to solve food shortages, but in fact implies the need for a far more humane solution.

102. SARCASM

Related to irony, sarcasm is acerbic in tone and strongly or mockingly condemns that which it appears to approve: for example, the sarcastic riposte 'Oh well done!' to something which is clearly not well done. Sarcasm relies to a great extent on tone and context for its effect, but since it is not a factual use of language it can be regarded as figurative.

103. INVECTIVE

A vehement accusation or renunciation. It is the opposite of irony and sarcasm in that it is direct rather than indirect, e.g.

I cannot but conclude the bulk of your natives to be the most pernicious race of little odious vermin that nature ever suffered to crawl upon the surface of the earth.

(Jonathan Swift)

104. FIGURATIVE STYLES OF WRITING

There are some styles of writing such as satire and parody, which are related to irony. A satire is a literary work in which topical issues, folly or evil etc. are held up to scorn by means of a mocking mimicry. For example, in the fourth book of *Gulliver's Travels*, Swift satirizes the follies and pretensions of humanity by means of the animalistic Yahoos.

In a parody the style of one work is humorously or mockingly copied by another. For example in *Northanger Abbey* Jane Austen parodies the style and form of contemporary Gothic novels.

105. FIGURATIVE USES OF WORDS

A very cursory examination of a few pages of a dictionary is sufficient to reveal the extraordinary number and variety of meanings that may be attached to a particular word. In the course of long use, words tend to develop new meanings, sometimes far removed from the original one. Many such changes have come about through a perception of the likeness between things. Thus the word *eye* originally meant the organ of vision; then, because of obvious resemblances, the name was also given to the eye of a needle, the eye of a potato etc. Similarly *foot*, originally the name of a part of the body, has been applied also to the foot of a mountain, the foot of a tree, the foot of a page.

In the instances quoted above, the name of one concrete thing has been transferred to another concrete thing that has some resemblance. But the extension of meaning is often carried further than this. We perceive a likeness between a material object and an abstract quality or condition, and then transfer the name of the material object to the abstraction. We speak, for instance, of the key to a problem, because just as a key unlocks a door, so some new fact or idea enables us to overcome a difficulty. The meanings of verbs have been extended in a similar way. Thus *boil* denotes, in its first sense, the action of a liquid under the influence of heat; but we also use the expression 'she was boiling with indignation', for there is an obvious resemblance between her condition and the condition of a heated liquid. In this way a figurative or metaphorical sense arises out of the original or literal meaning of a word.

Common errors

106. WORDS OF SIMILAR FORM BUT DIFFERENT MEANING

Listed below are pairs of words which are often confused. Examples and brief definitions are provided to help differentiate between the words given.

Adverse—averse
Adverse refers to something which is contrary to what is expected or desired, whereas *averse* means unwilling or reluctant to do something.
 In spite of the adverse weather conditions, the match went ahead as planned.
 Although she was very conscientious, she was not averse to taking days off.

Affect—effect
Affect means to act on or influence, whereas *effect* means to cause to happen or to achieve.
 He would have effected his escape without difficulty, but the noise he made affected his plan.

Alternate—Alternative
Alternate means to occur or cause to occur successively or by turns, whilst *alternative* suggests a possibility of choice between two things.
 You can return to this hospital on alternate days (every other day) or you can seek alternative medicine (another form).

Apposite—opposite
Apposite means pertinent to or relevant, whilst *opposite* means entirely different or situated directly facing.
 Since we were discussing something very different, his remark was not very apposite.
 He ran straight out of the front door and into the house opposite.

Appreciative—appreciable
Appreciative means expressing gratitude, admiration or respect. *Appreciable* means sufficient to be easily seen, measured or noticed.
 The pianist was so sensitive that he could only play to appreciative audiences.
 There is no appreciable difference between these two shades of green.

Beneficent—benevolent
Beneficent means generous or charitable in a practical context, whilst *benevolent* refers to character or disposition, and means friendly or pleasant.
 His huge income allowed him to be extremely beneficent to his home town.
 Though he was very poor he still maintained a benevolent disposition.

Canvas—canvass
Canvas is a fabric. To *canvass* is to solicit votes, orders, advertising etc.
 The tent is made of canvas.
 He has to canvass for orders.

Compliment—complement
A *compliment* is a form of praise, whilst a *complement* is a thing which makes something else complete, or it is the complete thing itself.

He was pleased at the compliment paid to him.

At first it was difficult to find sailors, but eventually the ship left port with a complement of men.

Contagious—contiguous

Contagious refers to the spreading of disease through contact. Things which are *contiguous* are in contact along a side or boundary and are therefore physically adjacent.

Smallpox is a contagious disease.

France and Germany are contiguous countries.

Contemptuous—contemptible

The former means showing or feeling contempt, while the latter means deserving contempt.

He was a proud man, contemptuous of those he considered his inferiors.

Her arrogance made her contemptible to those around her.

Credible—creditable—credulous

Credible means capable of being believed, *creditable* means praiseworthy, and *credulous* means tending to believe something on little evidence.

To nobody else did the story seem credible.

His behaviour in such circumstances was very creditable.

He is so credulous that he immediately believed my story of a ghost.

Defective—deficient

The former means not working properly, the latter means lacking something important.

The plane came to grief because of a defective engine.

He fails as a novelist because he is deficient in imaginative power.

Deprecate—depreciate

To *deprecate* means to express disapproval of, while to *depreciate* means to lessen the value of something through criticism, or to decline in value or price.

I strongly deprecate the substitution of abuse for argument.

Some newspaper critics seem to depreciate every book which comes under their notice.

A currency is said to depreciate when its purchasing power decreases.

Dominant—dominate—domineer

Dominant is an adjective which describes the action of a force which *dominates* (verb), i.e. has control. To *domineer* is to wield power through arrogance or tyranny.

Blue was dominant in the colour scheme.

By sheer force of character she was able to dominate the situation.

The bully likes nothing better than to domineer over weaklings.

Effective—effectual—efficient

Effective means capable of producing a result, *effectual* means capable of producing a particular intended result, and *efficient* means functioning properly without waste.

Owing to the shortage of teachers, the intentions of the GCSE will not become effective for several years.

He could find no effectual remedy for his complaint.

The firm needed a really efficient head to reorganize it.

Exceedingly—excessively
Exceedingly refers to something which is very great or of an unusual degree, while *excessively* refers to something which is of too great a degree.

He was an exceedingly obliging man, always willing to help those around him.

She was an excessively humble woman, unable to stand up for herself.

Expedient—expeditious
Expedient means suitable for a situation, or appropriate. *Expeditious* means done with speed or efficiency.

Although such a decision was against her principles, she found it expedient to give way when she was out-voted.

He found it necessary to use the most expeditious means possible of reaching the hospital with his pregnant wife.

Illegible—ineligible
Illegible refers to writing which cannot be deciphered. *Ineligible* means not fit for or not qualified for something.

That handwriting is illegible; no one can read it.

Owing to his youth, he was ineligible for the post.

Imaginary—imaginative
Imaginary means existing in the imagination and, therefore, unreal. *Imaginative* means produced by or indicative of a creative imagination.

He continually worries himself about imaginary ailments.

The greatest poets show very highly developed imaginative powers.

Industrial—industrious
Industrial means having or concerning industries; *industrious* means hard-working.

Liverpool was once a heavily industrial area, but now many of its factories have closed down.

She was very industrious and always completed her work on time.

Industrial—industrious
Industrial means having or concerning industries; *industrious* means hard-working.

Liverpool was once a heavily industrial area, but now many of its factories have closed down.

She was very industrious and always completed her work on time.

Judicious—judicial
Judicious means wise, while *judicial* refers to the administration of justice.

The England manager made a judicious selection for the game.

Despite the years they had spent in prison, they claimed they were innocent victims of the judicial system.

Luxuriant—luxurious
Luxuriant describes that which is rich and abundant. *Luxurious* means characterized by luxury.

Owing to the great heat and moisture, the vegetation in the tropics is extremely luxuriant.

We sat down to a luxurious banquet.

Negligent—negligible
Negligent means lacking in proper care and attention. *Negligible* means so slight as to be unimportant.

He was dismissed because he was negligent in his work.
The difference between the twins was so slight as to be negligible.

Notable—notorious

Notable means worthy of note, while *notorious* means well known for an unfavourable quality or deed.

The discovery of radium was a notable stage in the development of science.
Pol Pot was notorious for his callousness.

Official—officious

Official means relating to an office or authority. *Officious* means unnecessarily ready to offer services or advice.

The news became known through an official communication.
He repeatedly offered his services where they were not wanted, until his chief told him not to be so officious.

Practice—practise

Practice is the noun, *practise* the verb, which refer to the customary repetition of an action.

Proficiency will come through practice.
I must practise playing the piano.

Precipitate—precipitous

To *precipitate* means to cause to happen sooner than expected. *Precipitous* means steep.

Think before you act; to precipitate action will lead to disaster.
The mountain is so precipitous that it cannot be climbed.

Primary—primitive

Primary refers to the first in importance or position, while *primitive* is characteristic of an early state or situation.

Better education is our primary aim if progress is to be made.
Primitive man used stone implements.

Principal—principle

Principal means first in importance or rank, or the head of an organization etc. A *principle* is a standard rule of conduct.

The principal person present was the head-teacher.
He was hoping to meet the Principal of the University.
I do not understand the principle on which this fax machine works.

Punctual—punctilious

Punctual means prompt or at the correct time, while *punctilious* refers to a scrupulous attention to correctness.

In spite of his long journey, he was always punctual in arriving at work.
She was most punctilious in performing the smallest duties attaching to her post.

Salutary—salubrious

The former means promoting an improvement, while the latter means conducive to health or wholesomeness.

The improvement in his conduct proved that he had learned a salutary lesson.
There are several spa towns in the south of England which claim to be the most salubrious spot in the country.

Stimulus—stimulant

A *stimulus* is anything which acts as an incentive. A *stimulant* is any substance which increases physiological activity.

He was so lazy that only the stimulus of poverty made him work.

The use of artificial stimulants is banned in most sports.

Transitive—transitory

Transitive is a grammatical term referring to verbs. *Transitory* means of a short duration.

A transitive verb is one denoting an action that is exerted on an object.

Human life is transitory compared to the life of the universe.

Vocation—avocation

A *vocation* is an inclination towards a specific career. An *avocation* is a minor occupation undertaken as a diversion.

Teaching is a vocation rather than a profession, even more so in recent years because of the relatively poor salaries.

In his spare time he pursues the avocation of gardening.

107. CERTAIN WORDS FREQUENTLY MISUSED

Care should be taken to avoid the incorrect use of the following words

Aggravate

This verb is used colloquially as a synonym for 'to annoy' or 'to exasperate'. It should not be so used in writing. Its true meaning is 'to increase the gravity of', 'to make worse'.

His illness was aggravated by the bad weather.

Differ

To *differ* must not be confused with 'to vary'; that is, it must not be followed by 'according to'. We say 'this colour differs from that', 'I differ from your opinion', 'however much you try to convince me, we shall always differ'; but it is incorrect to say, 'the value of leisure differs according to a person's daily occupation'. Substitute 'varies' for 'differs'.

Disinterested

Often confused with *uninterested*. To be disinterested in a matter is to be without self-interest in it, to be impartial and detached, whereas to be uninterested means to have no interest.

Exotic

This does not mean 'luxurious' or 'lavish'. Its proper sense is 'introduced from abroad', and it is applied to fashions, words, plants etc.

Factor

A *factor* is one of the elements, circumstances or influences that contribute to a result. It must not be used unless the notion of contributing to a result is present.

Education is an indispensable factor in national progress.

Idea

This word is colloquially used in sentences such as 'that's a good idea', 'I don't understand the idea of this machine', 'the idea has received much support', 'his idea was to gain possession of the money'. In formal writing it is best to guard against making *idea* serve for 'plan', 'principle', 'cause' or 'scheme'.

Individual

This word must not be used as a synonym for 'person'. An individual is a single person, as opposed to a group. The following examples illustrate correct usage:

In a despotic state, absolute power is in the hands of an individual.

If the majority of the individuals in a state prosper, does the state as a whole prosper?

When *individual* is correctly used, a contrast between a single person and a group is always implied.

Indulge in

This should only apply to pleasures or amusements. It should not be extended as a replacement for 'engage in'. Used intransitively, *indulge* means 'to take one's pleasure freely'.

Infer

This is sometimes wrongly used for 'imply'. It is incorrect to say, 'The last sentence of his letter infers that he has resigned from his media-sales post.' But we could correctly say, 'I infer from the last sentence that he has resigned.'

Job

This is an overused word in colloquial English. It is frequently used in place of 'post', 'appointment', 'task' etc.

The latter

Through failure to construct sentences with sufficient care, writers frequently resort to the expedient of using *the latter*, as in the following example:

The facility, speed and cheapness with which books and newspapers can be printed, and the astonishingly short time in which news is given to the public have proved a great boon to the latter.

Here *the latter* is meaningless, since it should refer to the second of two persons or things, whereas several things have previously been mentioned. It is a sound rule never to use *the latter* unless it is in conjunction with *the former*.

Literally

When we say that a statement is literally true, we mean that it is not to be understood figuratively or metaphorically. *Literally* is not to be used as a synonym for *completely*. The word is often misused as in the following:

Two hundred and fifty of the new hundred-seater 'jumbo-buses' are to be put on the streets in the coming months. It is believed that they will literally eat up waiting crowds.

Obviously 'eat up' is meant to be taken metaphorically; hence *literally* is absurdly inappropriate.

Minimize

This means to reduce to a minimum.

We have taken all precautions to minimize the risk of accidents.

It is often wrongly used to mean 'underestimate'.

Mostly

An overworked word in colloquial language. Common examples of misuse are as follows:

(a) Lorries are now mostly used for the transport of heavy goods.

(b) This programme is mostly watched by adults.

In (a), 'mostly' should be replaced by 'generally'; in (b), it is misplaced since it should come immediately before the phrase to which it refers, 'by adults'. (See p. 38.)

Mutual

Mutual means reciprocal and is sometimes incorrectly used in place of *common*, as in the title of Dickens's novel *Our Mutual Friend*. For a relationship to be mutual, A must be doing to B as B does to A. In Dickens's title, let A and B be the persons indicated by 'our', and C 'the friend'. No reciprocal relationship exists between A and B but only a separate relationship between each of them and C.

The following are examples of correct usage:

The two party leaders found it to their mutual interest to form a coalition.

They could not work together successfully because of their mutual suspicion.

Nice

In colloquial language this word is used as a substitute for many different adjectives: a nice hat, a nice mess, a nice man, a nice taste etc. It has thus acquired such a vague meaning that it should be avoided in writing. Use the precise adjective required by the context.

Non-success etc.

Compounds with *non-* are frequently found in clumsy writing. They should be avoided if a synonym can be found which avoids the *non-* prefix.

Percentage

This is often used instead of 'number' or 'proportion'. This word obviously belongs to the sphere of mathematical calculations and is quite inappropriate in a context such as: 'A large percentage of the congregation paid no attention to the sermon.'

Protagonist

This word originally meant the chief actor in a drama or story. It has also come to be used for a leading person in a struggle for some cause.

Boris Yeltsin is the protagonist in the campaign for radical reform in the USSR.

It is incorrect, however, to use it to mean an advocate or supporter of an idea or scheme; and it is obviously wrong to speak of 'the chief protagonist', for the idea of 'chief' is contained in the word itself.

Substitute

The two idioms 'substitute for' and 'replace by' are often confused. When A is removed and B is added in its place, we say that A is replaced by B, or B is substituted for A. It is wrong to say that A is *substituted by* B.

Transpire

This is often loosely used for 'happen' or 'occur'; its proper, figurative meaning is to become known, to come to light.

Unique

If we say a thing is unique, we mean, strictly, that there is nothing precisely similar to it in existence. *Unique* is thus a word that is not often applicable. When used, it must not be qualified by an adverb as 'rather unique', 'very unique': a thing is either unique or not unique.

Other adjectives that do not admit of comparison are *square*, *golden*, *round*, *universal* and *preferable*. To say 'quite (square etc.)' is to use the word 'quite' unnecessarily. We can, however, say 'nearly square', for this is a possibility. Although we cannot have degrees of squareness, we can have degrees of approach to squareness.

Glossaries

108. SYNONYMS AND ANTONYMS

(a) Synonyms are words that have almost the same meaning:
battle, conflict, conquest
colour, dye, paint, stain, tinge
acute, keen, sharp

It may be said that no two words in English have exactly the same meaning and usage. Sometimes pairs of words are found that seem identical in meaning, but closer study will reveal some distinction not at first apparent. If we take *begin* and *commence*, for instance, we notice that *commence* belongs to more formal language than does *begin* which, being a simpler word, has a much wider usage. Again, *rich* and *wealthy*, though apparently identical in meaning, are not really so. *Wealthy* is restricted in its application to persons having a great deal of property or money, but *rich* has many applications, for example 'rich jewellery', 'rich soil', 'rich in suggestions'.

(b) Antonyms are words that have opposite meanings:

young–old	extricate–involve
rich–poor	deprive–endow
friend–enemy	sever–connect
fast–slow	consider–ignore
bright–dull	fluent–laboured
negligent–careful	beautiful–ugly

(c) Important synonyms
The creative use of synonyms to express subtleties of meaning is one of the hallmarks of a good style. The following list, while not exhaustive, will repay study as it suggests the variety in English vocabulary. A dictionary will help explain the different nuances of each related word. Note, where the first word in the series has both a primary and a secondary meaning, these meanings are distinguished by being numbered (1) and (2) respectively.

aberration, wandering, deviation
absolute, not relative, unconditional, unrestricted, unalterable
abstruse, recondite, hidden, difficult (to understand)
accessory, additional, auxiliary, aiding
achieve, accomplish, gain, perform
acme, summit, highest point
acquiesce (in), assent (to), rest satisfied
adept (at), proficient, skilled
adequate, competent, sufficient
adherent, partisan, follower
adhesive, sticky
adventitious, accidental, casual
aggravate, make worse
alleviate, make light, mitigate, relieve
ameliorate, make better, improve
antithesis, contrast
apathy, want of feeling, indifference
aphorism, maxim, apophthegm

appalling, terrifying, dreadful
apposite, apt, suitable
appraise, value, estimate
apprehend, (1) seize, arrest, (2) know, fear
arbitrary, without law, despotic, absolute
basic, core, fundamental, elementary
boredom, ennui, monotony, tedium
brown, chestnut, auburn, tan, tawny
busy, occupied, engaged, employed
cadaverous, corpse-like, pallid, gaunt
cajole, persuade, flatter
calumny, detraction, slander
candid, sincere, ingenuous, straightforward
captious, censorious, hypercritical
casual, (1) chance, irregular, (2) offhand, relaxed
catastrophe, disaster, calamity
category, class
charlatan, impostor, mountebank, quack
chicanery, trickery
choleric, irascible, petulant
cogent, powerful, convincing
colossal, gigantic
condign, merited, appropriate
consequent (upon), following, resulting
consequential, arrogant, pompous
contingent (on) (adj.), conditional, uncertain; (noun) batch, group
contumely, disrespect, insolence, rudeness, abuse
conversant (with), familiar
criterion, standard, test, rule
crucial, testing, decisive, very important
cursory, hasty, superficial, careless
cynical, sceptical, sneering, misanthropic
damp, moist, soggy, wet
darken, dim, obscure, overshadow
decent, proper, fitting, appropriate
definitive, complete, final, authoritative
desultory, fitful, irregular, rambling
deteriorate, grow worse
didactic, moralizing, instructive
diffident, modest, bashful
dissipate, (trans.) scatter, waste; (intrans.) disperse, disappear
domestic, (1) home, household, (2) tame, housetrained
dream, vision, illusion, hallucination, fancy
earn, gain, get, obtain
eccentric, irregular, strange, idiosyncratic
economy, (1) management of money, (2) judicious expenditure, frugality
edible, eatable, wholesome
effete, exhausted, decadent, worn out
effrontery, audacity, boldness, impertinence
egotism, conceitedness
elicit, draw out, give rise to
emaciated, lean, skinny
emulate, imitate, rival
enervate, deprive of nerve, weaken

ephemeral, transient, short-lived
eradicate, destroy
exacerbate, embitter, aggravate, provoke
exculpate, absolve, vindicate
exigency, necessity, emergency, distress
exiguous, meagre, slender
extravagant, unrestrained, excessive, wasteful, showy
fancy, (1) imagine, conjecture, (2) desire
fascinate, charm, enchant
fashion, (noun) vogue, convention, (verb) make, create
fastidious, dainty, over-nice
fatuous, silly, purposeless
fellow, (1) man, boy, (2) companion, associate
flagrant, notorious, scandalous, blatant
flood, inundate, submerge, overwhelm
fortuitous, chance, accidental
foul, dirty, wicked, rainy
foundation, (1) basis, groundwork, (2) establishment
garrulity, loquacity, talkativeness
genre, category, type
grandiose, pretentious, flamboyant
green, (1) verdant, grassy, (2) emerald, (3) new, immature, (4) jealous
handsome, (1) good-looking, attractive, (2) generous
harvest, crop, produce, results
hate, detest, loathe, abhor, dislike
heart, core, centre, soul, passion, tenderness, courage
heretical, unorthodox, iconoclastic
hunger, appetite, emptiness, famine, longing
hypocrisy, insincerity, deceit
illicit, unlawful, clandestine
illiterate, unlearned, ignorant
immaculate, (1) spotless, (2) innocent, guileless
immature, (1) unripe, (2) inexperienced, childish
imminent, threatening, impending
imperative, authoritative, obligatory, vital
impertinent, (1) irrelevant, (2) impudent, insolent
implacable, inexorable, irreconcilable, merciless
inaccessible, unapproachable
inception, beginning
indict, arraign, accuse
indigent, poor, destitute
indite, write
inexorable, resolved, relentless, inflexible, unalterable
innocuous, harmless, inoffensive
insidious, treacherous, false, cunning, stealthy, wily
journey, voyage, trip
judicious, wise, prudent, sensible
juvenile, young, adolescent, immature
juxtaposition, contiguity, contact, adjacency
ken, knowledge, awareness, scope
kin, relations, relationship
kindness, benevolence, charity, philanthropy, tenderness
laconic, concise, pithy
ludicrous, laughable, ridiculous

lugubrious, mournful, sorrowful, dismal, sombre
morbid, diseased, unhealthy, pessimistic
moribund, dying
naive, ingenuous, artless, innocent
naughty, bad, wicked, mischievous, gullible
nice, pleasant, agreeable, enjoyable, fastidious
nonsense, rubbish, drivel, stupidity
nugatory, (1) trifling, (2) insignificant, ineffectual, futile
obliterate, erase, destroy
obloquy, (1) censure, calumny, (2) disgrace
obsequious, servile, excessively compliant
obtuse, (1) blunt, (2) dull, stupid
onerous, burdensome, oppressive
ovation, triumph, applause, acclamation
panegyric, eulogy, encomium
penury, want, poverty
perdition, ruin, loss, damnation
peremptory, authoritative, firm
permeate, pass through, pervade
perspicacity, insight, perceptiveness, sagacity
perspicuity, clearness, lucidity, precision
pertinacious, obstinate, persevering
plagiarism, (literary) theft
plebeian, proletarian, vulgar, popular
precarious, uncertain, perilous
precocious, advanced, forward
predilection, partiality, inclination
prescience, foreknowledge, foresight
promulgate, publish, proclaim
quite, (1) completely, entirely, perfectly, (2) rather, moderately
quixotic, impractical, unrealistic, fanciful
rapacious, greedy, predatory, ravenous
recrimination, counter-charge, calling names
recuperate, recover (intrans.)
red, crimson, scarlet, ruby, vermilion
reimburse, refund, repay
reiterate, repeat
relevant, pertinent, related, appropriate
repudiate, reject, disclaim, disavow
reticent, silent, reserved
satiate, satisfy, glut, cloy
sedative (adj.), calming, soothing
sedulous, persistent, diligent, constant
shibboleth, watchword, slogan
solicitude, anxiety, care
spurious, false, specious, imitation (adj.)
supposititious, false, imaginary
sycophant, flatterer
taciturn, morose, silent
tentative, experimental, essaying, hesitant
tortuous, (1) twisted, winding, (2) deceitful, devious
transpire, become public
ubiquitous, being everywhere
unique, standing alone, single, unequalled

urbane, polite, courteous, refined
vacillate, waver, hesitate
voracious, greedy
wanton, (1) lewd, libidinous, (2) needless, gratuitous
wholesome, healthy, hygienic, good
yarn, (1) tale, story, (2) thread, fibre
zeal, fervour, enthusiasm
zenith, peak, culmination

109. IDIOM

Idiomatic language is that which follows the patterns of the everyday discourse of native speakers. In every language there are hundreds of combinations of words, often used figuratively and each having a special significance, which it is very difficult for the foreigner to understand because s/he has no similar expression in his/her own language. Note, for instance, the following English phrases containing the word *break*:

break one's fall	break step
break away	break the ice
break wind	break the bank
break new ground	

The correct and easy use of idiomatic expressions is one of the essential requirements of a good prose style.

(a) Here is a brief list of some idiomatic phrases; each phrase is defined and is accompanied by at least one sentence demonstrating how the phrase is employed idiomatically.

Black sheep
A person who is bad or not up to the usual standards of the others in a group.
> My brother is a lawyer and my sister is a doctor, but as an actor I'm the black sheep of the family.

Horse sense
Common sense.
> He was not well educated but his horse sense enabled him to progress in a big City firm.

Look a gift horse in the mouth
To question that which is freely offered.
> You might not like your lawyer, but since he offers the work for free you should not look a gift horse in the mouth.

A house of cards
An idea or system which is likely to fail.
> His exam failure caused his career plans to collapse like a house of cards.

The curate's egg
Something which is unsatisfactory in most parts but not all.
> The car was like the curate's egg; fast, but expensive to run.

To brush beneath the carpet
To hide or ignore something unpleasant.
> Only by brushing the affair under the carpet was the Cabinet Minister able to diminish the repercussions of his illegitimate child.

An eye for an eye (a tooth for a tooth)
A punishment or form of retribution which is as violent or as cruel as the original act.

The death penalty for murderers is a primitive, eye for an eye form of justice.

Sit on the fence
To make no clear choice between two opposing sides or options.

Voting for the third party can be either a belief in centrist politics or just sitting on the fence.

Flash in the pan
Something which lasts or is popular for only a very short time.

They have never been top of the league before. Is theirs to be a long-term success or is it just a flash in the pan?

A part of the furniture
A person who is taken for granted because s/he has been in a place for a long time.

That man has come into this pub every night for the past three years and he has become a part of the furniture.

Guinea pig
A person who is used as a subject for medical or other experiments.

When I was a student I was so poor I let the hospital use me as a guinea pig, as long as they paid me.

Give or get the sack
To dismiss or be dismissed from a job or appointment.

He was late so often for work that we had to give him the sack.

Take with a pinch of salt
To doubt that something is completely true.

You have to take his stories about seeing UFOs with a pinch of salt.

(b) Idiomatic use of prepositions
Mistakes frequently arise through the wrong use of prepositions after certain words. The following are examples of correct usage:

His conduct does not *accord with* that of a man in his position.
I *acquiesce in* her decision.
Such conduct does not *admit of* excuse.
I do not *agree with* his opinion (or with him).
I do not *agree to* her proposal.
His disease was *aggravated by* the bad climate.
He is not *amenable to* discipline.
He is greatly *averse to* doing it.
She is *chary of* admitting her mistakes.
She is not *cognizant of* the facts.
Such conduct is not *compatible with* the law.
He *connived at* their misconduct.
Confusion was *consequent on* the end of the war in Cambodia.
He is *deficient in* tact.
She would not say anything *derogatory* even *to* her enemies.
This is *different from* mine.
He showed a marked *distaste for* politics.
She is *guiltless of* any intention to harm him.
He becomes *impatient with* anyone who interrupts him.
He is *impatient of* any interruption.

A raincoat must be made of material that is *impervious to* water.
Measles is a disease especially *incidental to* childhood.
She likes to be *independent of* all assistance.
This remark was *indicative of* her whole outlook.
He is *ineligible for* the job *on account of* his youth.
I can *exercise* no *influence over* my son.
He *has* considerable *influence with* the Prime Minister.
He is *inspired by* the struggle.
The principles were *instilled into* him in his youth.
I do not wish to *intrude on* you.
She acted thus *irrespective of* all my wishes
His extreme views will *militate against* his success.
He showed himself to be very *negligent of* his duty (or *in* carrying out his duty).
He talked on, quite *oblivious of* her presence.
This course of action is *preferable to* that one.
His arrogance is *prejudicial to* his job-chances.
She was *preoccupied with* other affairs.
His closest friend could not *prevail upon* him to stay.
No one can hope to *prevail against* such overwhelming odds.
She was *profuse in* offers of assistance.
The USA and the USSR have only recently been *reconciled with* each other.
He soon became *reconciled to* life on the dole.
He gives notice that he will not be *responsible for* his son's debts.
The Government should be *responsible to* the people.
I am not *satisfied with* my present job.
I am not *satisfied of* the truth of what you say.
His remarks *savour of* hypocrisy.

(c) Incorrect idioms

Idioms are often incorrectly used because of the confusion of two similar phrases. For example:

The sit-com was so funny we nearly died with laughter.
The correct idiom is 'died of'.

After a thorough search they gave it up as lost.
'Gave up for lost' is correct.

(d) Idiomatic expressions and their peculiarities

Idiomatic expressions sometimes seem to break the accepted rules of grammar, but they are not necessarily to be discarded on this account. We can say, 'the play acted so admirably that the author's fame was assured.' Here the active verb *acted* is used in a passive sense (the play was admirable when it was acted). Idioms often preserve words and meanings of words that have now passed out of use, for example 'to bear in mind'. Here *mind* really means memory, which was the original meaning. There are many idiomatic phrases whose origin cannot be traced; yet they are frequently used, for example to beat hollow; the bitter end.

(e) Foreign idioms

The English language contains many idioms that are literal translations of idiomatic phrases from French, Latin or other languages. A few examples are:

As for me–Quant à moi
Everyone to his taste–Chacun à son goût
In any case–En tout cas
In passing–En passant
That is to say–C'est à dire
Wonderful to relate–Mirabile dictu

110. LOAN WORDS

English contains many words which are straight, untranslated borrowings from other languages. These words and phrases are borrowed for several different reasons. They may owe their origin to some foreign form of sport or pastime which has become popular in this country. Often they denote a sense of pretension or snobbery which calls for the use of exotic language. They may, however, fill a semantic gap in existing English and thereby increase the wealth of the English vocabulary. The list below supplies some of the most frequently used loan words. The language of origin is indicated as follows:

Ar. – Arabic	It. – Italian
F. – French	Jap. – Japanese
G. – German	L. – Latin
Gr. – Greek	Rus. – Russian
Hin. – Hindi	Sp. – Spanish

à bas [F.]. Down! down with!

à bientôt [F.]. See you again soon.

ab initio [L.]. From the beginning.

Achtung! [G.]. Attention!

ad astra [L.]. To the stars.

à demi [F.]. By halves.

à deux [F.]. For two people only.

ad hoc [L.]. For this particular purpose, specially.

ad infinitum [L.].To infinity.

ad nauseam [L.]. So as to disgust or nauseate.

ad rem [L.]. To the point.

advocatus diaboli [L.]. The devil's advocate.

affaire d'honneur [F.]. An affair of honour, a duel.

à gogo [F.]. In abundance.

aide-mémoire [F.]. A memorandum, an aid to memory.

à jamais [F.]. For ever.

à la [F.]. According to; in the style of.

à la carte [F.]. By the bill of fare.

à la mode [F.]. In fashion.

al dente [It.]. Cooked, but still firm when bitten.

al fresco [It.]. In the open air.

allons! [F.]. Come, let us be off!

Alma Mater [L., fostering mother]. One's school, college or university.

alter ego [L.]. One's second self.

amende honorable [F.]. Public apology, public amends.

à merveille [F.]. Admirably, perfectly.

amicus curiae [L.]. A friend of the court, an adviser with no personal interest.

amour-propre [F.]. Self-esteem, vanity.

anno Domini [L.]. In the year of our Lord.

annus mirabilis [L.]. A year of wonders.

ante bellum [L.]. Before the war.

ante meridiem [L.]. Before noon.

à outrance [F.]. To the end, to extremities.

à pied [F.]. On foot.

à plaisir [F.]. At pleasure, at will.

a posteriori [L.]. From effect to cause; inductive.

apparatchik [Rus.]. A civil servant, bureaucrat.

après-ski [F.]. The evening's social activities after a day's skiing.

a priori [L.]. From cause to effect; deductive.

argumentum ad hominem [L.]. An appeal to personal interests etc.

arrivederci [It.]. Goodbye.

ars longa, vita brevis [L.]. Art is long, life short.

artium magister [L.]. Master of Arts.

assez bien [F.]. Moderately well.

à tout prix [F.]. At any price.

à travers [F.]. Across, through.

au contraire [F.]. On the contrary.

au courant de [F.]. Fully informed about.

au fait [F.]. Familiar, well-acquainted with.

au fond [F.]. At bottom.

auf Wiedersehen [G.]. Goodbye.

au gratin [F.]. (Cooked) with bread-crumbs or grated cheese.

au naturel [F.]. In its natural state.

au pied de la lettre [F.]. Literally, precisely.
au revoir [F.]. Till we meet again.
au sérieux [F.]. Seriously.
Autobahn [G.]. A motorway.
autostrada [It.]. A motorway.
aux armes! [F.]. To arms!
avant-propos [F.]. Preface, preliminary remarks.
à votre santé! [F.] To your health!

Bachelier ès lettres, sciences [F.]. Bachelor of Letters, of Science.
ballon d'essai [F.]. A feeler.
batterie de cuisine [F.]. A set of cooking utensils.
beaux esprits [F.]. Men of wit.
beaux yeux [F.]. Fine eyes, good looks.
bel esprit [F.]. A brilliant mind, man of parts.
ben trovato [It.]. Well invented.
ben venuto [It.]. Welcome.
bête noire [F.]. A bugbear, one's aversion.
bien aimé [F.]. (*fem.* **aimée**) Well-beloved.
bien entendu [F.]. To be sure, of course.
blague [F.]. Humbug.
Blitzkrieg [G.]. Lightning war, a sudden and devastating attack.
bona fide [L.]. In good faith.
bonjour [F.]. Good day.
bon marché [F.]. A bargain; cheaply.
bon mot [F.]. A witty saying.
bonne-bouche [F.]. A dainty morsel.
bonsoir [F.]. Good evening.
bon ton [F.]. Fashion, good style.
bon vivant [F.]. One fond of good living.
bon voyage [F.]. A pleasant journey, farewell.
bureau de change [F.]. An office for exchanging currency.

ça ira [F.]. That will go, that's the thing.
canaille [F.]. The rabble.
carpe diem [L.]. Enjoy the day, seize the present opportunity.
carte blanche [F.]. (Unlimited) freedom of action.
casus belli [L.]. A reason for war.
cause célèbre [F.]. A notable case or trial.

cela va sans dire [F.]. That goes without saying.
ce n'est que le premier pas qui coûte [F.]. It is only the first step that is troublesome.
c'est-à-dire [F.]. That is to say.
c'est la vie [F.]. That's life.
chacun à son goût [F.]. Every one to his taste.
chef-d'oeuvre [F.]. A masterpiece.
chemin de fer [F.]. A railway.
cherchez la femme [F.]. Look for the woman, there's a woman at the bottom of it.
che sarà, sarà [It.]. What will be, will be.
ciao [It.]. An informal expression of greeting or farewell.
ci-devant [F.]. formerly, of a past time.
cinéma vérité [F.]. A realistic, documentary style of cinema.
circa [L.]. About.
cogito, ergo sum [L.]. I think, therefore I exist.
comme il faut [F.]. As it should be, correct.
communiqué [F.]. An official report.
compos mentis [L.]. Sound of mind.
compte rendu [F.]. An official report.
con amore [It.]. With affection, with zeal.
con spirito [It.]. With animation.
coup de grâce [F.]. A finishing stroke.
coup de main [F.]. A sudden attack, enterprise or undertaking.
coup d'état [F.]. A stroke of policy; a sudden, esp. unconstitutional, change of government.
coup d'oeil [F.]. A rapid glance.
coûte que coûte [F.]. Cost what it may.
crème de la crème [F.]. The very best.
cri de coeur [F.]. An appeal or utterance from the heart.
cui bono [L.]. For whose advantage?
cum privilegio [L.]. With privilege.

d'accord [F.]. Agreed; in time.
dacha [Rus.]. A country house.
dame d'honneur [F.]. A maid of honour.
de bonne grâce [F.]. With good will, willingly.
de facto [L.]. In reality, actually.

défense de fumer [F.]. Smoking not allowed.

dégagé [F.]. (*fem.* **dégagée**) Informal, casual; uncommitted.

Dei gratia [L.]. By the grace of God.

déjà vu [F.]. (The illusion of) already having seen something one is in fact seeing for the first time.

dejeuner à la fourchette [F.]. A fork lunch.

de jure [L.]. By right.

de luxe [F.]. Luxurious.

demi-tasse [F.]. A small coffee-cup.

Deo gratias [L.]. Thanks be to God.

Deo volente [L.]. God willing.

de profundis [L.]. Out of the depths.

de rigueur [F.]. According to strict etiquette.

dernier ressort [F.]. A last resource.

de trop [F.]. Superfluous, not wanted.

deus ex machina [L.]. A god from the machine (in the Gr. theatre), a romantic *dénouement.*

deux-chevaux [F.]. A small two-horse-power car, especially a Citroën.

dies irae [L.]. The Day of Judgment.

Dieu et mon droit [F.]. God and my right.

Dieu vous garde! [F.]. God protect you!

dolce far niente [It.]. Sweet idleness.

dolce vita [It.]. The sweet life (of comfort and idleness).

Domine, dirige nos [L.]. O Lord direct us (the motto of the City of London).

Dominus illuminatio mea [L.]. The Lord is my light (the motto of Oxford Univ.).

Dominus vobiscum [L.]. The Lord be with you.

dum spiro, spero [L.]. While I breathe, I hope.

ecce homo [L.]. Behold the man!

echt [G.]. Genuine.

édition de luxe [F.]. A sumptuous edition.

embarras de richesse [F.] A superfluity of anything wanted or desirable.

éminence grise [F.]. A grey eminence, a person exercising power behind the throne.

en arrière [F.]. In the rear, behind.

en avant [F.]. Forward.

en bloc [F.]. In the mass.

en déshabillé [F.]. In casual dress; in one's true colours.

en effet [F.]. Substantially, in effect.

en famille [F.]. With one's family, at home.

enfant terrible [F.]. A precocious youngster.

en fête [F.]. In festivity.

engagé [F.]. (*fem.* **engagée**) (Politically) committed.

en garçon [F.]. As a bachelor.

en grande tenue [F.]. In full dress.

en masse [F.]. In a body.

en passant [F.]. By the way.

en rapport [F.]. In sympathy with.

en règle [F.]. In order, as it should be.

en revanche [F.]. In return, as compensation.

en route [F.]. On the way.

en suite [F.]. In a set, in succession.

entente cordiale [F.]. A good understanding.

entre nous [F.]. Between ourselves, in confidence.

e pluribus unum [L.]. One out of or composed of many (motto of the USA).

esprit de corps [F.]. loyalty to and pride in one's school, regiment etc.

et tu Brute! [L.]. And thou too Brutus (the last words of Caesar).

ex cathedra [L.]. From the chair, with authority.

ex gratia [L.]. As an act of favour.

ex officio [L.]. By virtue of one's office.

ex post facto [L.]. After the deed is done.

façon de parler [F.]. Manner of speaking.

fait accompli [F.]. An accomplished fact.

faites vos jeux [F.]. Place your bets.

far niente [It.] Doing nothing.

fatwa [Ar.]. A Muslim religious decree.

faute de mieux [F.]. For lack of anything better.

faux pas [F.]. A blunder, a slip.

fecit [L.]. He (or she) made or drew it.

fiat lux [L.]. Let there be light.

fidei defensor [L.]. Defender of the faith.

fille de chambre [F.]. A chambermaid.

floreat [L.]. May (it) flourish.

fonctionnaire [F.]. A civil servant, clerical worker.
force majeure [F.]. Superior power, circumstances not under one's control.
Franglais [F.]. French which contains a high proportion of English words.
fruits de mer [F.]. Seafood, shellfish.

garde du corps [F.]. A bodyguard.
gardez bien [F.]. Take good care, be careful.
gens d'affaires [F.] Business people.
glasnost [Rus.]. Openness and accountability of government.
gloria in excelsis Deo [L.]. Glory to God in the highest.
gloria Patri [L.]. Glory be to the Father.
Glühwein [G.] Mulled wine.
grâce à Dieu [F.]. Thanks be to God.
grande passion [F.]. A serious love-affair.
guru [Hin.]. A Hindu spiritual teacher.

hara-kiri [Jap.]. Ceremonial suicide by disembowelling.
Hausfrau [G.]. A housewife.
Heimweh [G.]. Homesickness.
homme d'esprit [F.]. A wit, a genius.
honi soit qui mal y pense [F.]. Shame be to him who thinks evil of it (motto of the Order of the Garter).
honoris causa or **gratia** [L.]. For the sake of honour, honorary.
hors concours [F.]. Without a rival.
hors de combat [F.]. Disabled.

ich dien [G.]. I serve (Prince of Wales's motto).
idée fixe [F.]. A fixed idea, monomania.
il n'y a pas de quoi [F.]. There is no need, don't mention it.
il va sans dire [F.]. It goes without saying.
in articulo mortis [L.]. At the moment of death.
in camera [L.]. In the judge's chamber, not in open court.
inconnu [F.]. (*fem.* **-nue**) Unknown.
in excelsis [L.]. In the highest.
in extremis [L.]. At the point of death.
in flagrante delicto [L.]. In the very act.
infra dignitatem (infra dig.) [L.]. Beneath one's dignity.

in loco parentis [L.]. In the place of a parent.
in medias res [L.]. Into the very middle of the business.
in memoriam [L.]. To the memory of.
in nomine [L.]. In the name (of).
in propria persona [L.]. In one's own person.
in re [L.]. In the matter of.
in saecula saeculorum [L.]. For ever and ever.
in situ [L.]. In (its original or proper) position.
inter alia [L.]. Among other things.
in toto [L.]. Entirely.
in vacuo [L.]. In a vacuum, in empty space.
in vino veritas [L.]. Drunkenness makes a person let out the truth.
ipso facto [L.]. By the fact itself.

je ne sais quoi [F.]. I know not what, something indefinable.
je suis prêt [F.]. I am ready.
jeunesse dorée [F.]. Gilded youth.
jihad [Ar.]. A holy war.

le beau monde [F.]. The world of fashion, society.
les convenances [F.]. The proprieties.
l'état, c'est moi [F.]. I am the State.
l'inconnu [F.]. The unknown.
lingua franca [L.]. A common language used for communication between people of different nationalities.
luge [F.]. A sledge.

magnum bonum [L.]. A great good.
magnum opus [L.]. A great undertaking, the great work of a person's life.
maître d'hôtel [F.]. A head waiter.
mala fide [L.]. In bad faith, treacherously.
mal à propos [F.]. Inappropriately.
mal de mer [F.]. Seasickness.
mal entendu [F.]. Misunderstood.
mañana [Sp.]. Tomorrow.
mardi gras [F.]. Shrove Tuesday.
marque de fabrique [F.]. A trademark.
mauvais ton [F.]. Bad style.
mea culpa [L.]. By my fault.
memento mori [L.]. An emblem or reminder of death.

ménage à trois [F.]. A household consisting of a husband and wife, and the lover of one of them.

mens sana in corpore sano [L.]. A sound mind in a sound body.

mise en scène [F.]. The production, or the setting, of a play.

mon Dieu! [F.]. Good heavens! gracious!

mot juste [F.]. The appropriate word or phrase.

moyen âge [F.]. The Middle Ages.

multum in parvo [L.]. Much in little.

mutatis mutandis [L.]. The necessary changes being made.

ne plus ultra [L.]. Nothing further; perfection.

nil desperandum [L.]. Never despair.

n'importe [F.]. It is of no consequence.

noblesse oblige [F.]. Rank imposes obligations.

non compos mentis [L.]. Not of sound mind, mentally deranged, lunatic.

non sequitur [L., it does not follow]. An illogical inference; an irrelevant conclusion.

nota bene [L.]. Note well.

nous avons changé tout cela [F.]. We have changed all that.

nous verrons [F.]. We shall see.

nouveau riche [F.]. (*pl.* **nouveaux riches**) A newly-rich man, a parvenu.

objet d'art [F.]. An art-object.

oeuvres [F.]. Works.

omnia mutantur, nos et mutamur in illis [L.]. All things are subject to change, and we change with them.

omnia vincit amor [L.]. Love conquers all things.

onus probandi [L.]. The burden of proving.

ora et labora [L.]. Pray and work.

ora pro nobis [L.]. Pray for us.

orate pro anima [L.]. Pray for the soul (of).

O tempora! O mores! [L.]. Alas for the times and the manners!

parbleu! [F.]. An exclamation of surprise etc.

par excellence [F.]. Pre-eminently.

par exemple [F.]. For instance.

pari passu [L.]. At the same rate or pace.

parole d'honneur [F.]. Word of honour.

pas de deux [F.]. A dance for two.

pas possible! [F.]. Impossible!

pas seul [F.]. A dance for one person.

pax Romana [L.]. The peace of the Roman Empire.

pax vobiscum [L.]. Peace be with you.

per annum [L.]. Yearly, by the year.

per contra [L.]. On the contrary.

perestroika [Rus.]. (Political and economic) reconstruction.

per se [L.]. By itself.

persona (non) grata [L.]. An (un)acceptable person.

pièce de résistance [F.]. The most important or best item.

pied-à-terre [F.]. A footing, a temporary lodging.

pis aller [F.]. A makeshift.

plat du jour [F.]. A dish of the day, not part of the usual menu.

plein air [F.]. The open air.

plus ça change [F.]. The more things change (the more they stay the same).

post obitum [L.]. After death.

pour ainsi dire [F.]. So to speak.

pour encourager les autres [F.]. To encourage the others.

pour faire rire [F.]. To raise a laugh.

preux chevalier [F.]. A brave knight.

prima facie [L.]. At first sight.

primus inter pares [L.]. First among equals.

pro bono publico [L.]. For the public good.

pro forma [L.]. As a matter of form.

pro rata [L.]. In proportion.

pro tempore [L.]. For the time being.

quelque chose [F.]. Something, a trifle.

que voulez-vous? [F.]. What would you have?

quid pro quo [L.]. Something in return.

qu'importe? [F.]. What does it matter?

qui s'excuse, s'accuse [F.]. He who excuses himself accuses himself.

qui va là? [F.]. Who goes there?

quod erat demonstrandum (QED) [L.]. Which was to be proved.

quod vide (q.v.) [L.]. Which (thing) see.

quo jure? [L.]. By what right?

quo modo? [L.]. By what means?
quo vadis? [L.]. Whither goest thou?

raison d'être [F.]. The reason for a thing's existence.
reductio ad absurdum [L.]. Proof by demonstrating the absurdity of the contrary.
répondez s'il vous plaît (RSVP) [F.]. Please reply.
requiescat in pace (RIP) [L.]. May s/he rest in peace.
revenons à nos moutons [F.]. Let us return to our sheep, let us come back to our subject.

samizdat [Rus.]. Clandestine, small-scale publishing of banned literature.
sans doute [F.]. Doubtless.
sans pareil [F.]. Unequalled.
sans peur et sans reproche [F.]. Without fear and without blame.
sans souci [F.]. Free from care.
sauve qui peut [F.]. Save himself who can.
savoir faire [F.]. Tact, skill.
semper eadem [L.pl.]. (*sing.* **idem**) Always the same.
Senatus Populusque Romanus (SPQR) [L.]. The Roman Senate and People.
se non è vero, è ben trovato [It.]. If it is not true, it is cleverly invented.
sic transit gloria mundi [L.]. So earthly glory passes away.
s'il vous plaît [F.]. If you please.
sine die [L.]. Without any day (being fixed).
sine qua non [L.]. An indispensable condition.
son et lumière [F., sound and light]. An entertainment using music, commentary and lighting to show the story of a historic building.
statim [L.]. At once.
Sturm und Drang [G.]. Storm and stress.
sub judice [L.]. Under consideration.
sub poena [L.]. Under penalty (of).
succès d'estime [F.]. A success with more credit than profit.
sui generis [L.]. Of its (his or her) own kind.
sui juris [L.]. Of his (or her) own right.

tabula rasa [L.]. A smooth tablet ('a clean slate').
taedium vitae [L.]. Weariness of life.
tant mieux [F.]. So much the better.
tant pis [F.]. So much the worse.
tempus fugit [L.]. Time flies.
terra incognita [L.]. An unknown land.
tour de force [F.]. A feat of strength or skill.
tout à coup [F.]. Suddenly.
tout à fait [F.]. Wholly, entirely.
tout à l'heure [F.]. Instantly.
tout de suite [F.]. Immediately.
tout ensemble [F.]. The general effect.

Übermensch [G.]. A superman.
ultra vires [L.]. Beyond one's (legal) powers.
urbi et orbi [L.]. To the city and the world.

vade in pace [L.]. Go in peace.
veni, vidi, vici [L.]. I came, I saw, I conquered.
verbatim [L.]. Word for word.
verboten [G.]. Forbidden.
verbum satis sapienti (verb. sap.) [L.]. A word is enough to the wise.
vers libre [F.]. Free verse.
via media [L.]. A middle course.
visagiste [F.]. An expert in facial make-up.
vivat rex (regina)! [L.]. Long live the king (queen)!
vive la République! [F.]. Long live the Republic!
vive l'Empereur! [F.]. Long live the Emperor!
voilà [F.]. See there, there it is.
voilà tout [F.]. That's all.
vox (*pl.* **voces) populi** [L.]. The voice of the people, popular feeling.
vox populi vox Dei [L.]. The voice of the people is the voice of God.

Weltgeist [G.]. The world-spirit.
Weltschmerz [G.]. World-sorrow, pessimism.
wunderbar [G.]. Wonderful.
Wunderkind [G.]. An infant prodigy, a whiz-kid.

Zeitgeist [G.]. The spirit of the age.

Part Three: Style

The sentence

The grammatical structure of sentences of various types, and the rules governing the relationship of the parts of a sentence to one another, are dealt with in Part One of this book. For the purposes of original composition the sentence must be considered as a means of expression; it must be regarded not as an isolated unit but as part of a continuous passage; and the relationship between its meaning and its form must be investigated.

111. UNITY

The first requirement of a good sentence is unity; that is, it must express only one main idea. It may contain more than one fact, but all the facts stated must have some relation to the central idea. The following sentences are faulty because they lack unity:

(1) The patrons of the bar were all tanned and expensively dressed and most of them worked in the City.

(2) Everton, one of our oldest football teams, was a founder member of the Football League and occupies a fine stadium in Liverpool.

In (1) the first part of the sentence states a fact about the appearance of the people, while the second part mentions their occupation. These totally different ideas should not be brought together in one sentence. Similarly in (2), we have two unrelated ideas, one concerning history and the other concerning location.

The following sentence, although a long one which contains several clauses, does not violate the rule of unity:

One morning, while he sat busied in those speculations which afterwards astonished the world, an old female domestic, who served him for a housekeeper, brought him word that an elderly gentleman and his daughter had arrived in the village the preceding evening, on their way to some distant country, and that the father had been suddenly seized in the night with a dangerous disorder, which the people of the inn where they lodged feared would prove mortal; that she had been sent for, as having some knowledge in medicine, the village surgeon being then absent; and that it was truly piteous to see the old man, who seemed not so much afflicted by his own distress as by that which it caused to his daughter.

All the numerous facts stated in this sentence are brought clearly into relationship with the central theme – namely, the message brought by the old servant.

112. LOOSE AND PERIODIC SENTENCES

Sentences are divided into two classes according to the arrangement of their parts. When the qualifying phrases or clauses are stated first and the main statement is kept until the end, the sentence is said to be periodic (or a period). A sentence is said to be loose if the main statement comes first and qualifying phrases or clauses follow.

The following are examples of periodic sentences.

Whether the Labour party, irrespective of its good showing in recent opinion polls, will be able to defeat the Tories in the next general election, depends upon its ability to overcome internal divisions.

In the Lenin Barracks in Barcelona, the day before I joined the militia, I saw an Italian militia man standing in front of the officers' table. (George Orwell)

These are examples of loose sentences.

This could have occurred nowhere but in England, where the men and the sea interpenetrate, the sea entering into the life of most men, and the men knowing something or everything about the sea, in the way of amusement, of travel, of bread-winning. (Joseph Conrad)

In the meantime he had been diligently preparing for the approaching interview with his boss by persuading his colleagues to intercede on his behalf, and to place his recent conduct in the most favourable light.

113. USES OF THE TWO TYPES OF SENTENCE

Of the two kinds of sentence, the loose is the more common and the more natural, since in expressing our thoughts we have a strong tendency to state our main idea first and to add our qualifications afterwards. In the periodic sentence we have an artificial structure designed to hold the reader's attention by keeping the meaning in suspense until the end. Periodic structure is a characteristic feature of dignified prose, whereas loose sentences are preferred by writers who adopt a more easy conversational or realistic style. A judicious mixture of the two types is desirable if agreeable variety is to be attained in ordinary prose.

114. CONVERSION OF LOOSE SENTENCES INTO PERIODS

Loose sentences may be converted into periods by rearrangement of the clauses. The following are examples.

It is clear that the ardent politician would never undergo the labours and make the sacrifices he does, did he not believe that the reform he fights for is the one thing needful. (LOOSE)

If the ardent politician did not believe that the reform he fights for is the one thing needful, it is clear he would never undergo the labours and make the sacrifices he does. (PERIODIC)

Very few are prepared to accept nuclear installations in their own neighbour-hood, although many are ready to endorse the importance of such places to the country's industry. (LOOSE)

Although many are ready to endorse the importance of nuclear installations to the country's industry, very few are prepared to accept such places in their own neighbourhood. (PERIODIC)

115. EMPHASIS

In order to bring out clearly the point of a sentence it is often necessary to give emphasis to a particular word or group of words. This may be done in various ways, of which the following are the chief.

(a) Parallel Structure

In order to give effectiveness to a sentence as an expression of a thought, writers frequently make use of the device of parallel structure; i.e. they give two or more parts of the sentence a similar form so that the whole has a definite pattern. The parallelism of structure is obvious in such a sentence as the following, in which we have a series of subordinate statements all beginning with 'What with . . .', leading up to the conclusion.

> What with perceptions unnaturally dulled by early thwarting, and a coerced attention to books – what with the mental confusion produced by teaching subjects before they can be understood – what with making the pupil a mere passive recipient of others' ideas, and not in the least leading him to be an active inquirer or self-instructor – and what with taxing the faculties to excess; there are very few minds that become as efficient as they might be.

Consider the following sentence:

> Along with political despotism, stern in its commands, ruling by force of terror, visiting trifling crimes with death, and implacable in its vengeance on the disloyal, there grew up an academic discipline similarly harsh – a discipline of multiplied injunctions and blows for every breach of them – a discipline of unlimited autocracy upheld by corporal punishment.

Here the noun 'despotism' is qualified by four parallel adjective phrases; similarly 'discipline', which is repeated twice, has its adjectival qualifications attached to it. The adjuncts of discipline are balanced against those of despotism.

Note how the parallel structure in the following serves to emphasize the contrast between 'rules' and 'motives'.

> It was not by furnishing philosophers with rules for performing the inductive process well, but by furnishing them with a motive for performing it well, that he conferred so vast a benefit on society.

One other example may be given:

> If we examine the geography of Britain, we shall find wealth in the south and poverty in the north; prosperous new towns established close to the capital, traditional industries decaying in the northern cities, and a population wishing to stay north, though forced to migrate south.

Here 'wealth' and 'poverty' are balanced against each other as are 'north' and 'south'. Moreover 'new towns', 'industries' and 'population' are all qualified by participial phrases; and forcible contrast is obtained at the end by the balanced phrases 'wishing to stay' and 'forced to migrate'.

From these examples it will be seen that not only does balanced structure give additional point to a sentence, but it also tends to produce an agreeable rhythm, which is an essential quality in good writing.

(b) Change in the natural order of words

It is to be noted that the most emphatic positions in a sentence are the beginning and the end – the beginning because it is the part that first strikes the ear, and the end because it is the climax. Now if certain words are taken out of their normal position and are place at the end or at the beginning of a sentence, they attract attention and are thus given emphasis. Consider these sentences:

> However difficult it is for the imagination to realize, it is a fact that men and women lived in luxury and refinement, practising the arts and cultivating letters, indulging in severe physical exercise, and building structures which had an elaborate system of drainage, four thousand years ago.

The normal position of 'four thousand years ago' would be after 'lived', but the writer wishes to emphasize these words, so he has put them at the end of the sentence, where they form the climax.

> Silver and gold have I none, but such as I have give I unto thee.

Here the natural order would be 'I have no silver and gold', but emphasis is secured by inverting the order of the subject and object. Similarly, 'I give' is inverted in the second clause.

> Ill though she was, she persevered until she had completed the work.

> Flash'd all their sabres bare,
> Flash'd as they turned in air,
> Sabring the gunners there.

Note the inversion of order of 'ill' and 'flashed' in the sentences above.

(c) Repetition
Repetition of some words or phrases is sometimes made use of for the purpose of emphasis.

> Scrooge was his sole executor, his sole administrator, his sole assign, his sole residual legatee, sole friend, and sole mourner. (Charles Dickens)

> More and more, because of this our blind faith in machinery, because of our want of light to enable us to look beyond machinery to the end for which machinery is valuable, this and that man, this and that body of men, all over the country, are beginning to assert and put in practice an Englishman's right to do what he likes; his right to march where he likes, meet where he likes, enter where he likes, hoot as he likes, threaten as he likes, smash as he likes. (Matthew Arnold)

(d) Use of correlative conjunctions (i.e. those that are used in pairs)
A sentence may be made more pointed by the use of correlatives. The sentence, 'He said that he wanted them to listen to what he had to say and to act upon it,' might be made more emphatic thus:

> He said that he wanted them not only to listen to what he had to say, but also to act upon it.

The following sentences furnish further examples.

> I considered that treasure rather as a possession to be secured, than as a prize to be contended for.

> By adhering in this manner and on those principles to our forefathers, we are guided not by the superstition of antiquarians, but by the spirit of philosophic analogy.

> He would have led his followers, not only to the verge, but also to the heart of the promised land. He would not merely have pointed out, but would have divided the spoil. Above all, he would have left, not only a great but a spotless name.

(e) The use of *It is, It was* as introductory phrases
Take the sentence

> My brother told you another story.

To emphasize 'my brother' we may write

> It was my brother who told you another story.

To emphasize 'another story' we may write

> It was another story that my brother told you.

(f) Balance and antithesis
It has been shown above how sentences may be made more forceful by the use of balanced phrases and clauses. To a special kind of balance is given the name antithesis. Antithesis is obtained by balancing contrary ideas or terms so as to produce an effective contrast, as in the following examples:

> People who never look backward to their own mistakes will not look forward to good fortune.

Here 'forward' is opposed to 'backward', and 'good fortune' to 'mistakes'.

> Thus, by preserving the method of nature in the conduct of the state, in what we

improve we are never wholly new; in what we retain we are never wholly obsolete.

God made the country and man made the town.

116. VARIETY IN SENTENCE STRUCTURE

The preceding examples call attention to the fact that a given idea may be expressed in sentences of varying form. A further example may be given to reinforce this point. Consider the following statement:

Their journey was safe and speedy, and they arrived late in the evening in London.

Without changing the sense it could be rendered in the following ways:

After a speedy and safe journey they arrived late . . ..

They made a speedy and safe journey, and arrived . . ..

Having made a speedy and safe journey, they arrived . . ..

If emphasis is to be placed upon the lateness of their arrival, we could say

Although their journey was speedy and safe, it was late in the evening when they arrived . . ..

In spite of a speedy and safe journey, it was not until late in the evening that they arrived . . ..

In a single sentence like the one above there may not seem to be any reason for preferring one form to another. It is when a sentence is considered, not as an isolated unit, but as part of a connected passage, that the possibility of variations in its construction becomes important. It must then be treated according to the nature of the statements that precede and follow it. A succession of short, grammatically simple sentences, or of sentences all having the same opening, or of longer sentences built on the same plan, will tend to produce monotony and flatness of style. Of course, the series of short sentences, like hammer-strokes, has its uses. Equally the long, more complicated sentence has its necessary place in, for instance, a piece of argument or difficult explanation. In ordinary writing, however, it will be found that variety in both the length and the form of sentences helps to give interest and vitality to the style.

The paragraph

In any long passage of prose the sentences are divided up into groups called paragraphs. Each paragraph begins with a fresh line, and this line is usually indented. A paragraph is a group of sentences that all help to express one idea. The rules for the construction of paragraphs are analogous to those governing the construction of a sentence.

117. UNITY

Like a sentence, a paragraph must have unity: that is to say, every sentence in it must have a definite relation to the main topic. If it can be said that any one sentence in a paragraph does not contribute towards the expression of the central idea, that paragraph is faulty. It should always be possible to express in a single sentence the theme of a well-constructed paragraph.

118. TOPIC-SENTENCES

We frequently find that the topic of a paragraph is more or less fully indicated in one of the sentences. The sentence indicating the theme is called the topic-sentence. We have seen, in dealing with loose and periodic sentences, that the main statement may come either at the beginning or at the end of the sentence. Similarly in paragraphs the theme may appear in the first sentence, to be followed by other sentences amplifying or illustrating it, or it may be reserved for statement in the last sentence, after reasons and illustrations have been given. Which of these two methods is chosen depends upon the effect the writer is aiming at.

The topic-sentence is found more commonly at the beginning than at the end, since in this position it engages attention, and the reader is enabled to grasp immediately what the leading idea of the passage is. Here is a simple example of a paragraph having a topic-sentence at the beginning.

When I was a boy almost everyone wore boots. Some were buttoned and some were laced, and I remember a great-aunt who wore the elastic-sided variety. Men wore the kind with a row of studs at the top round which to twist the lace, and a loop at the back with which to tug them on to the feet in the hurried minutes after breakfast. In some houses there was still to be seen screwed into the floor a curious kind of iron clutch called a boot-jack, into which paterfamilias stuck the heel of his boot to remove it when he came home in the evening. Women and girls wore rather high laced or button boots and there was much use of an almost obsolete weapon called a button hook. Boys wore boots that were not so high and usually laced. No children would have been allowed to wear sandals. (*The Times*)

The paragraph opens with the general statement that in the writer's boyhood almost everyone wore boots. The following sentences expand on the idea of 'everyone' by referring in detail to men, women, girls, boys and children.

Another example of this form of paragraph structure may be given.

Apart from weapons there was a shortage of the minor necessities of war. We had no maps or charts, for instance. Spain has never been fully surveyed, and the only detailed maps of this area were the old military ones, which were almost all in the possession of the Fascists. We had no range-finders, no telescopes, no periscopes, no field-glasses except a few privately owned pairs, no flares or Very lights, no wire-cutters, no armourers' tools, hardly even any clearing materials. The Spaniards seemed never to have heard of a pull-through and looked on in surprise when I constructed one. When you wanted your rifle cleaned you took it to the sergeant, who possessed a long brass ramrod which was invariably bent and therefore scratched the rifling. (George Orwell)

The topic-sentence stating the shortage of the minor necessities of war comes first. The following sentences work out this fact in detail.

It is extremely important that a paragraph should exhibit coherence. The facts and ideas should be arranged in logical order, and there should be an easy transition from sentence to sentence. The sequence of thought may be kept clear by the judicious use of connectives such as 'however', 'moreover', 'again', 'on the other hand', 'above all', 'in conclusion'.

Attention to coherence is especially necessary when the paragraph is long, otherwise the reader will find it difficult to keep track of what is being said. The following is an example of a fairly long paragraph characterized by the smooth flow of ideas. Observe the use of connectives which are italicized.

Words cannot be formed to express the endless varieties of the Venetian sunset. The most magnificent follow after wet stormy days, when the west breaks suddenly into a labyrinth of fire, when chasms of clear turquoise heavens emerge, and horns of flame are flashed to the zenith, and unexpected splendours scale the fretted clouds, step over step, stealing along the purple caverns until the whole dome throbs. *Or again*, after a fair day, a change of weather approaches, and high, infinitely high, the skies are woven over with a web of half-transparent cirrus clouds. These in the afterglow blush crimson, and through their rifts the depth of heaven is of a hard and gemlike blue, and all the water turns to rose beneath them. I remember one such evening on the way back from Torcello. We were well out at sea between Mazzorbo and Murano. The ruddy arches overhead were reflected without interruption in the waveless ruddy lake below. Our black boat was the only dark spot in this sphere of splendour. We seemed to hang suspended; and such as this, I fancied, must be the feeling of an insect caught in the heart of the fiery-petalled rose. *Yet not* these melodramatic sunsets *alone* are beautiful. *Even more* exquisite, perhaps, are the lagoons, painted in monochrome greys, with just one touch of pink upon a western cloud, scattered in ripples here and there on the waves below, reminding us that day has passed and evening come. *And* beautiful *again* are the calm settings of fair weather, when sea and sky alike are cheerful, and the topmost blades of the lagoon grass, peeping from the shallows, glance like emeralds upon the surface. There is no deep stirring of the spirit in a symphony of light and colour; but peace, purity, and freshness make their way into our hearts. (J. A. Symonds)

Here again the topic-sentence comes first. We see that the paragraph is to deal with the 'endless varieties of the Venetian sunset'. The remainder of the paragraph, in fact, amplifies the initial statement by giving descriptions of some of the typical varieties of sunset and by suggesting that there are many more whose beauty eludes description.

The following is an example of a paragraph in which the topic is reserved for the final sentence.

If every second of our lives recurs an infinite number of times, we are nailed to eternity as Jesus Christ was nailed to the cross. It is a terrifying prospect. In a world of eternal return the weight of unbearable responsibility lies heavy on every move we make. That is why Nietzsche called the idea of eternal return the heaviest of burdens. (Milan Kundera)

119. EMPHASIS

Just as emphasis is necessary to bring out the point of a sentence, so it must also be secured in the building up of a paragraph. The most important part of a paragraph, the topic-sentence, must be stressed, and its position in the paragraph is, therefore, the first consideration. It will gain emphasis if placed at the beginning, for it can then be developed throughout the rest of the paragraph; its position at the end can be equally emphatic if it acts as a fitting and striking climax to a series of ideas; and it may even be placed near the middle of a paragraph if the balance of the paragraph demands such an arrangement. If numerous subsidiary ideas are grouped in the topic-sentence, deal with these carefully and see that they do not oust the main idea from its prominent position.

It is often effective to make use of repetition in building up a paragraph, but such a device needs careful handling. Just as the use of parallel phrases and clauses is sometimes valuable in order to give force and rhythm to a sentence, so a similar device may occasionally be used to give point to the argument of a paragraph. A paragraph exhibiting parallel structure contains a series of sentences formed alike and illustrating the same idea. The following are examples:

It will be seen that we do not consider Bacon's ingenious analysis of the inductive method as a very useful performance. Bacon was not, as we have already said, the inventor of the inductive method. He was not even the person who first analysed the inductive method correctly, though he undoubtedly analysed it more minutely than anyone who preceded him. He was not the person who first showed that by the inductive method alone new truth could be discovered. But he was the person who first turned the minds of speculative men long occupied in verbal disputes, to the discovery of new and useful truth; and by doing so, he at once gave the inductive method an importance and dignity which had never belonged to it before. He was not the maker of the road; he was not the discoverer of that road; he was not the person who first surveyed and mapped that road. But he was the person who first called the public attention to an inexhaustible mine of wealth, which had been utterly neglected, and which was accessible by that road alone. (Thomas Babington Macaulay)

To be committed to that is nothing whatever to do with submission to anybody. It is the discovery of those social relationships which are in any case there. It is what I think Sartre meant by reverberation, resonance: the active consciousness of those social relationships which include ourselves and our practices. It is never likely to be a convenient discovery, in our kind of world. It permits very little in the way of being immediately signed up for somebody else's policy. But when it really happens, in the many different ways that are possible, its sound is usually unmistakable: the sound of that voice which, in speaking as itself, is speaking, necessarily, for more than itself. Whether we find such voices or not, it is worth committing ourselves to the attempt. (Raymond Williams)

It is possible to say that this device can easily be overworked, and then it is more likely to arouse antagonism than conviction. At the beginning of an argument, when logic and the gentlest persuasion are required, it would be useless; but it is effective, after conviction has been secured, to turn conviction into enthusiasm.

120. LENGTH OF PARAGRAPHS

There can obviously be no rigid rule about the length of paragraphs. One idea may be quite effectively stated in half a dozen lines; another one will perhaps need so much explanation and illustration that it will occupy half a page. Overly short paragraphs should be avoided; if an idea can be exhausted in two or three lines, it is not sufficiently important to be made the theme of a complete paragraph.

The essay

For the purposes of this book the term 'essay' can be defined as a short literary composition which treats a subject analytically or speculatively. The essay, so understood, may contain narrative or descriptive elements, but will also include comments and criticisms representing the writer's own point of view.

The difference between purely narrative or descriptive composition and the essay proper may be seen by a consideration of the two possible ways in which a subject like 'The Development of the Aeroplane' might be treated. The simpler treatment of this subject would be a narrative of the various stages in the development of the aeroplane, beginning with the early attempts at gliding and ending with the position reached at the present day. But a composition of this kind would not be a true 'essay'. The writer of a true essay on this theme would make use of the historical facts, but would subject them to criticism; s/he would appraise the value of the various achievements in aeroplane construction and would consider the possibilities of the future; in short, besides providing a statement of the facts the essay would give a revelation of the writer's own mind. The essay thus becomes an expression, not merely of knowledge, but of thought and imagination.

121. THE FOUR STAGES IN ESSAY-WRITING

A sensible approach to writing an essay is described in the following four stages:
(1) Think about the subject, and set down on paper all the facts or ideas that occur to you.
(2) Arrange these facts according to topics, and so construct an outline for the composition.
(3) Write the essay proper.
(4) Revise what you have written.

122. NOTES ON THE FOUR STAGES
(a) The title must be read carefully, so that the precise scope of the subject and the point of view from which it is to be treated may be grasped.

(b) When the facts have been arranged, it will be found that they group themselves under certain heads. Suppose there are five topics. Each of these topics will now form the subject of a paragraph, and the essay will contain five paragraphs in all. The rules of paragraph-structure should be carefully observed. It must be seen that a due proportion of space is allotted to each aspect of the subject.

(c) In writing the essay, one must pay attention, of course, to grammar, punctuation and style. In the matter of style the following points should be particularly noted.
(1) Clearness is the first essential: therefore words must be chosen accurately; words, phrases and clauses must be placed in the right order; all pronouns must be clear in their reference.
(2) Slang and colloquial expressions should be avoided, unless they are appropriate to the particular essay.
(3) The 1st person should not be used in any essay in which the subject can be treated impersonally: that is to say, such expressions as 'I think', 'in my opinion', must not be used. To qualify a statement it is always possible to use impersonal expressions such as 'it is generally agreed', 'it can be seen'.

(d) It is most important that everything that is written should be revised. In this way the writer will detect a number of errors which can easily be corrected, but which, if allowed to remain, would detract considerably from the value of the work. It cannot be too strongly emphasized that the actual writing of an essay is only half the task: the preliminary arrangement of the material and the final revision of the work are of great importance, and must receive careful attention if a good result is to be obtained.

123. COMMON ERRORS

The paragraphs of the essay should not be numbered.

Headings must not be inserted in the body of the essay.

Single sentence paragraphs should be avoided. In general, each paragraph should consist of several sentences.

124. PLAN AND COHERENCE OF IDEAS

We have already insisted on the need for a definite plan and for proper paragraphing in every essay. But even when the difficulty of structure has been mastered, there is still more to be learned before a good essay can be produced. In most essays there should be a clear line of thought or argument governing the arrangement of the material and giving coherence to the ideas.

125. ESSAYS OF DIFFERENT STYLE AND PURPOSE

(a) Narrative and descriptive essays

Many essays require the presentation of some form of factual knowledge, for example travel or historical writing. The simplest form of such an essay is where the material is ready to hand and only needs proper arrangement. For instance, if the topic were 'The Development of Aviation' the following is a specimen outline indicating how the material should be arranged:

The Development of Aviation

(1) Brief historical introduction: Early attempts to fly – balloons – the Wright brothers.

(2) Aviation as a practical means of transportation belongs to the twentieth century: Bleriot's crossing of the Channel – the development of airships.

(3) Aviation and the First World War: combatants quickly took advantage of the new weapon – struggle for air supremacy – military needs brought astonishing developments in aeronautical science.

(4) Aviation and the Second World War: still further mechanical and safety innovations – greatly increased speed, capacity and endurance – Battle of Britain.

(5) Post-war developments: jet engine – supersonic speed – great extension of passenger services – hijacking, air terrorism, space-shuttle.

However, this is just a starting-point for an analytical essay. Suppose the subject of 'Polar Exploration' is chosen. The production of a series of paragraphs written in good English and arranged according to some such plan as the following is not necessarily all that is required.

(1) The objects of the explorers.

(2) History of the early expeditions.

(3) Discovery of the North Pole by Peary, and of the South Pole by Amundsen.

(4) The tragedies of Scott and Shackleton.

(5) The trials of Fuchs and Hillary.

(6) More recent explorations and scientific implications.

But such a composition will not be a true essay if each paragraph is treated as an isolated unit having no connection with the one preceding it or the one following it, and having no clearly assignable place in a complete structure. An essay is not a mere collection of disjointed paragraphs: it must be considered as a whole, and each paragraph must be made to contribute to the overall effect. The first paragraph should lead on to the second, the second on to the third, and so on. This means, of course, that the opening and closing sentences of each paragraph must be carefully considered and constructed.

Now the best way to give coherence to the essay on 'Polar Exploration' would be to adopt some definite point of view and make the essay illustrate or justify it. Often the title indicates the point of view to be taken. Thus, the essay might be made to answer the question: 'Are polar expeditions worth the expense and the sacrifice?' Or the history of polar exploration might be considered as a remarkable manifestation of the spirit of adventure and discovery inherent in the human race. In this way, by keeping a leading idea in the mind throughout the composition, the writer will be able to produce a structure that is a unified whole, and not merely a conglomeration of disjointed fragments.

In another example, a travel essay written about Eastern Europe could be given a definite focus by connecting the simple facts of the travelogue to the political changes following the collapse of the Berlin Wall.

(b) Argumentative essays

Essay subjects frequently require the writer to discuss a certain problem and to present a logical statement of his/her point of view, for example 'The Dangers of Nuclear Power Stations', 'Simplified Spelling', 'The Politics of Censorship', 'Morality and Abortion'. In dealing with such questions the writer must first of all decide what his/her own point of view is to be, but this does not necessarily mean 'taking sides' or presenting only one point of view. Rather it means the exploration of the topic through a clear and consistent development of ideas.

The writer should generally arrange the essay so that the statement of personal opinion comes in the last paragraph. The preceding paragraphs should set out the argument leading to this conclusion. The opening paragraph will generally contain an explanation of the nature of the problem to be discussed.

Often the title for an essay of this kind consists of a quotation, for example 'East is East and West is West', 'Comfort is the aim of science'. It is important that the writer should not assume that such a quotation contains a statement of undoubted truth. It generally expresses either a half-truth or an opinion that invites discussion or opposition. It is the business of the essay-writer to say how much truth, if any, is contained in the statement, and to give reasons for the view that is put forward. It is generally inadvisable to adopt an extreme partisan attitude, especially when dealing with sensitive issues. As far as possible, both sides of the question should be stated. The following is a method of treatment for such an essay:

Comfort is the aim of science
Outline:
(1) Science gives us ample supplies of the necessities of life.
(2) It also supplies us with luxuries.
(3) It mitigates bodily ills.
(4) Yet it is not true to say that comfort is the aim of science.

A title of this kind is likely to trap the unwary. There is an obvious connection between science and comfort, but this must not blind the essay-writer to the fact that it is not true to say that comfort is the aim of science. The first three paragraphs of the essay are devoted to explaining the connection between comfort and science.

Since the last paragraph points out the fallacy of the title, it is the most important part of the essay, and needs the most careful handling. The final sentence sums up the whole argument. When one is writing an essay of this kind, it is of the utmost importance that the line of argument be kept clear, with easy transitions from one stage to the next. Notice how the opening and concluding paragraphs are constructed so as to carry on this sequence of ideas.

The following is an outline of an essay of similar type:

The case for modern architecture.
Outline:
(1) There is much criticism of modern architecture. Is such criticism justified?
(2) If we analyse the criticism, we find that it is not so much criticism of the architecture as criticism of its modernity. The majority are conservative, and therefore reluctant to applaud or even accept innovation.
(3) The architect, on the other hand, is an artist, and as such is searching for new ideas, new concepts, new methods, to express the spirit of the age.
(4) The industrialist who commissions the factory, or the individual who orders a bungalow, is financially entitled to make his/her own choice of building; but if s/he seeks the assistance of a twentieth-century architect, s/he must expect a design in the twentieth-century idiom.
(5) It is certainly reasonable to make informed criticisms of modern buildings as being poor of their kind, but it is unreasonable to criticize them simply because they are of their kind.

The title makes no statement, but suggests a subject for discussion. In dealing with this subject a definition of terms is desirable at the outset.

(c) Discursive essays
Often essays do not set out to prove a particular point but rather to discuss or interpret a specific theme or idea. The subject could be a quotation or proverb embodying an idea that will command general agreement. This idea is to be explained and illustrated. Examples are 'Knowledge is power' or 'Honesty is the best policy'.

In writing an essay of this kind, the writer faces the danger of making a mere catalogue of examples for and against the given argument. At the beginning, the meaning intended to be conveyed is explained, and after the enlargement via the examples in the second and third sections, the whole is rounded off by a general discussion, which refers to the earlier parts of the essay.

The following outline is an example of this type of essay.

The worst vices are often only a corruption of the best virtues.
(1) Introduction: Human nature is a web of mingled yarn – good and bad qualities inextricably mixed – the paradox that even virtues may become vices in special circumstances.
(2) Obvious examples of the lesser virtues which, carried to excess, become vices: frugality becomes meanness – excessive caution may result in complete lack of enterprise – generosity with money may pass into foolish recklessness.
(3) The great virtues also may be perverted into vices: a strong sense of justice, without imagination and sympathy, becomes evil in its effects – love for a child can become smothering – faith in a personal mission can become egotism.
(4) But does corruption of the 'best' virtues result in the 'worst' vices? The author of the dictum has, perhaps, sacrificed strict truth to the desire to make a striking antithesis.

126. ESSAY VOICE, STYLE AND TONE

The voice and style which are adopted by the essay-writer must be appropriate and consistent to the content. Style may be used to describe a particular type of writing distinguished by its function or context (e.g. legal style) or to refer to some general features of writing. In an academic context language is used to express analytical and abstract thinking. For this reason you will find lengthier and more complex sentences in an academic paper than in, say, an army instruction manual. The purpose of the manual is to issue instructions; lengthy, complex sentences are not the best means of doing this.

Let us tackle the matter of distinctive style by examining this paragraph from an academic journal:

What are the anatomical bones for the human communication system? Asymmetry of the brain has been linked with language and speed and was once considered a distinguishing feature of the human neocortex. But recent research shows that there is possible asymmetry in the cortex of great apes (orangutan and chimpanzees). Hemisphere symmetry implies specialization of function; coordination and integration, therefore, become critical. The size of the corpus callosum, a bundle of nerve-fibres connecting the right and left hemispheres, is consistent with the possibility of some hemispheric asymmetry for the great apes.

This paragraph is distinctly academic in its style. Its context and its use of specialist terms indicate this. Furthermore, the cautiousness with which claims are made ('But recent research shows . . . possible asymmetry . . .') adds to this. The tone of the passage is that of academic detachment. The writer is somewhat distanced from the material that is being evaluated; there is a definite concern for evidence and objectivity of tone, which can lead to some very long and complex structures. Consider the contrasting style of this passage:

I grant that high school classes are so large that marking for the average teacher of English is a monstrous burden. But I believe strongly that there should be at least one written assignment marked every fortnight of the high school teaching year. I do not believe that poor expression should be left unmarked in case the mark scar the pupil's psyche. I believe excellence should be encouraged positively, and ill-structured, ill-spelt and ill-punctuated writing strongly discouraged. No football coach tolerates constantly muffed passes. Why should we grant less respect to the greatest invention, language?

The tone of voice here is emotional and subjective. It is more of a polemic than an academic essay. The academic writer's approach to material should be analytical and objective, rather than subjective and emotional, and should make frequent use of passive forms of verbs and impersonal pronouns and phrases.

127. THE OPENING PARAGRAPH

The opening sentence should contain a noun referring to the title. Thus if the subject is 'Music', the essay should not begin, 'It is one of the oldest arts.' The word 'music' should be repeated.

It is most important to devise a good opening on an abstract theme; in fact, it may be said that writing the introduction is half the battle. Once a sound and perhaps original idea for our first sentence is struck upon, the remaining sections of the essay follow naturally. On the other hand, few essays recover from a lame and unfocused opening. It is, therefore, worth while spending considerable thought on the introductory paragraph. The writer should at once get rid of the notion that this section of the essay need be nothing more than a collection of disconnected sentences containing commonplace ideas that have only a vague connection with the subject. The opening should not, of course, be unduly abrupt, but it should introduce the reader to a perfectly definite idea bearing on the theme. For example, Umberto Eco, writing on 'The World Cup and its Pomps', begins thus:

> Many malignant readers, seeing how I discuss here the noble sport of soccer with detachment and irritation, and (oh, all right) malevolence, will harbour the vulgar suspicion that I don't love soccer because soccer has never loved me, for from my earliest childhood I belonged to that category of infants or adolescents who, the moment they kick the ball – assuming they manage to kick it – promptly send it into their own goal or, at best, pass it to the opponent, unless with stubborn tenacity they send it off the field, beyond hedges and fences, to become lost in a basement or a stream or to plunge among the flavours of the ice-cream cart. And so his playmates reject him and banish him from the happiest of competitive events. And so suspicion will never be more patently true.

The beginning is striking in that a general issue is made relevant by the introduction of the writer's personal feelings. Robert Lynd has an essay on 'The Mouse'. At first sight this seems an umpromising title: its opening lines start in a banal, effusive manner: 'The mouse is a small rodent that lives either in the fields or in human habitations.' Lynd, however, has something original to say, and his next sentence puts the reader on the alert for the ideas that are to follow:

> It is an engaging problem in ethics whether, if you have been lent a cottage, you have the right to feed the mice. There will be for most people only one answer to the question. Your first duty, they will tell you, is to the man who has been good enough to lend you his house, and you must do nothing that would damage it or even annoy him if he knew about it. On the other hand, it is reasonable to argue that the feelings of a mouse who is present are more to be considered than the feelings of a host who is absent. Besides, he need never know anything about it. He may be surprised on his return to find mice running up the clock, mice cantering up and down the side of the fireplace, mice playing on the floor under the table, mice in his jam cupboard, mice nibbling the corners of the books on the lower shelves, mice, in fact, behaving as if the house were a vast restaurant for themselves and a crèche for their children. But, as he is a good man, he will put it all down to an accident, and never suspect that the people to whom he lent the cottage could have done anything so disgraceful as to actually scatter food on the floor and invite the mice of the neighbourhood to make themselves at home.

It is clearly impossible to prescribe rules for the opening of an essay, but some of the methods may be mentioned and exemplified.

(a) A striking opening sentence

We have seen that skilful essayists often aim at embodying a striking idea in the first paragraph. Such an opening can be made more effective if the first sentence is crystallized into a witty remark or an epigram. Here are some instances of such beginnings:

Bacon: 'Of Death':

> Men fear death as children fear to go into the dark.

Bacon: 'Of Gardens':

> God Almighty first planted a garden . . .

A forcible opening sentence may sometimes be obtained by quoting the voice of a well-known authority, for example, Hazlitt: 'On Manner':

> It was the opinion of Lord Chesterfield that manner is of more importance than matter . . .

Or the opening sentence can disagree with accepted opinion, for example, T.S. Eliot: 'Hamlet':

> Few critics have ever admitted that Hamlet, the play, is the primary problem, and that Hamlet, the character, is only secondary.

(b) An anecdote

An anecdote, provided it has a definite point connected with the topic in hand, will occasionally be found a useful method of opening. For example, this is the opening paragraph of Flannery O'Connor's essay 'King of the Birds':

When I was five I had an experience that marked me for life. Pathe News sent a reporter to Savannah to take a picture of a chicken of mine. This chicken, a half Cochin Bantam, had the distinction of being able to walk either forward or backward. Her fame spread through the press, and by the time she reached the attention of Pathe News, I suppose there was nowhere left for her to go – forward or backward. Shortly after that she died, as now seems fitting. If I put this information at the beginning of an article on peacocks, it is because I am always being asked why I raise them, and I have no reasonable answer.

(c) Definition of terms

It is sometimes desirable to define in the first paragraph one or more of the terms used in the title. For example Seamus Heaney, writing on English Pastoral Verse, begins:

'Pastoral' is a term that has been extended by usage until its original meaning has been largely eroded. For example, I have occasionally talked of the countryside where we live in Wicklow as being pastoral rather than rural, trying to impose notions of a beautified landscape on the word, in order to keep rural for the unself-conscious face of raggle-taggle farmland. And we have been hearing about Hardy and Hemingway as writers of pastoral novels, which seems a satisfactory categorization. Originally, of course, the word means 'of, or pertaining to, shepherds or their occupation', and hence a poem, play etc. in which the life of shepherds is portrayed, often in conventional manner: also extended to works dealing with country life generally.

However, it must be said that writers of essays tend to do this much more than is necessary. If you are writing on 'The Influence of the Cinema', it is not necessary to explain what the cinema is, or how and when it began: in the first place, you are concerned with the influence, and not with the cinema itself. On the other hand, if your subject is 'The Drawbacks of Civilization', it might be desirable to have an introductory statement defining civilization, since everybody has his/her own ideas about it and a definition prevents cross-purposes. Again, definition would probably be necessary in an essay on 'Romance', because this term is used in so many different senses. But before beginning an essay with a definition of terms, the writer should be quite sure that a definition is really necessary.

128. THE FINAL PARAGRAPH

As with the opening paragraph, so with the concluding paragraph, writers often experience difficulty. It is important to give an essay a graceful conclusion, and not to bring the reader to an abrupt halt. In some essays the last paragraph presents no difficulty: in an argumentative composition, for instance, the summing up and the statement of the writer's own opinion will naturally come at the end. Sometimes it is possible to conclude with a generalization suggested by the subject. Again, a quotation from some distinguished authority may fitly round off an essay.

It is best to avoid beginning the final paragraph with stereotyped phrases like the following:

In conclusion we may say . . .

Summing up, we see the advantages greatly outweigh the disadvantages . . .

Finally, looking at the matter from both points of view, we may conclude that . . .

Précis-writing

A précis is an abridgment or summary of the subject-matter, either of a single piece of writing or of a series of pieces on a topic. Its purpose is to present the gist of the piece or pieces in a clear and concise form, so that it can be easily understood and quickly assimilated. In the present chapter only précis of single passages will be dealt with.

129. GUIDELINES

(a) Condensation of sentences
In analysing sentences into clauses the reader has in effect extracted the main statement of the sentence every time he or she has picked the main clause. This principle may be applied to a whole passage containing a number of complex sentences; the chief statements will most probably be found in the major clauses, while the minor details will appear in the subordinate clauses.

In the example given below the précis-writer has reproduced the essential point of each sentence as briefly and as clearly as possible.

A land may be covered with historic trophies, with museums of science and galleries of art, with universities and with libraries; the people may be civilized and ingenious, the country may even be famous in the annals and actions of the world; but if the population every ten years decreases, the history of that country will soon be a history of the past.

Condensed statement:

Any nation, no matter how cultured and powerful it may be, will come to ruin if it is decreasing in numbers.

(b) Awareness of paragraph structure
The ability to pick out topic-sentences (p.98) and, therefore, to be aware of the essential point of the passage in hand is an important skill for the précis-writer to master.

(c) Summarizing by omission
Sometimes it is possible to make a fairly adequate summary of a passage by merely taking certain sentences or phrases and omitting the rest: the summary then appears in the actual language of the original passage.

130. ESSENTIAL FEATURES OF A GOOD PRÉCIS

(a) Content
The summary should contain all the important facts, and omit unimportant details. Conclusions, definite opinions etc. should be given. Reasons and arguments leading up to those conclusions or statements of opinion may often be left out; so also may illustrations and examples. But if, for instance, the original passage states at length a single argument leading up to one conclusion, the reasons, examples etc. will be important and will have to appear in the summary.

(b) Length
A précis should rarely be longer than one-third of the original passage. The précis should normally be contained in one paragraph.

(c) Form

Summaries of speeches and of dialogue should appear in indirect speech, i.e. they should be in the third person and the past tense; speeches should be introduced by some words such as 'The speaker said that . . .'. In all business précis-writing, also, and when the object of the précis is to preserve a summary or to serve as a record, the indirect (reported) form should be used. In a summary of a literary passage or article, the person and tense of the original may be retained.

(d) Language

The language and style of the summary should be simple and clear. Figurative language in the original should be reduced to plain, straightforward English in the summary. It is not necessary, however, to change all the original expressions merely for the sake of changing them. If a phrase in the original expresses an idea in the best possible way, it will naturally be retained.

(e) Order

The order of the various points will generally be the same in the précis as in the original, but when, as sometimes happens, the facts are badly arranged in the original, they should be rearranged in logical sequence. So long as the true purport of the original passage is preserved, any rearrangement that facilitates the required compression is legitimate.

(f) Connection of ideas

The connection of ideas should be kept clear. A précis of an argument should not consist of a series of short simple sentences apparently expressing a number of detached ideas. The transition from one idea to the next should be made easy by the judicious use of connectives.

131. METHOD

(a) The passage should be read sufficiently thoroughly to ascertain what the main topic is.

(b) A title should be formulated, and the main topic indicated in it.

(c) The passage should be read through again – this time slowly and carefully – and the important points to be included in the final précis should be underlined. A point is 'important' if it is essential to the adequate and clear exposition of the central theme.

(d) Brief notes of these points should be made. Copying out the language of the original should be avoided if the task in hand specifies the use of the writer's own words.

(e) From these notes, and without reference to the original, a continuous and grammatical summary of the passage should be written.

(f) The words in this summary should be counted. If it is too long, it should be shortened by the elimination of detail and the condensing of phraseology until it is of the length required. If that is too short, phraseology should be examined to ensure that the meaning is quite clear. The original should be referred to again to ensure that nothing important has been omitted.

(g) The draft précis should be compared to the original passage to make sure that the meaning of the original has been correctly rendered.

132. EXAMPLES

(a) Narrative
The following passage has been summarized in not more than one-third its original length:

> The first care of Nicuesa, on resuming the general command, was to take measures for the relief of his people, who were perishing with famine and disease. All those who were in health, or who had strength sufficient to bear the least fatigue, were sent on foraging parties among the fields and villages of the natives. It was a service of extreme peril; for the Indians of this part of the coast were fierce and warlike, and were the same who had proved so formidable to Columbus and his brother when they attempted to found a settlement in this neighbourhood.
>
> Many of the Spaniards were slain in these expeditions. Even if they succeeded in collecting provisions, the toil of bringing them to the harbour was worse to men in their enfeebled condition than the task of fighting for them; for they were obliged to transport them on their backs, and, thus heavily laden, to scramble over rugged rocks, through almost impervious forests, and across dismal swamps.
>
> Harassed by these perils and fatigues, they broke forth into murmurs against their commander; accusing him not merely of indifference of their sufferings, but of wantonly imposing severe and unnecessary tasks upon them out of revenge for their having neglected him. (Washington Irving)

Comments
A plain narrative is easily summarized. When the main facts have been selected, they must be stated briefly with due regard to the connection of one to another. The condensed statement must be presented in well-constructed sentences: it should not read like a series of scrappy notes.

Outline of précis
Relief of starvation – foraging parties – hardships and losses – murmurs against commander.

Précis
> Nicuesa's first aim was to secure provisions for his starving followers. All who were not incapacitated by disease were sent on the dangerous service of foraging. In these expeditions many Spaniards were slain by the warlike natives, and the remainder were so overcome by the toil of transporting food that they began to murmur against their commander and accuse him of wantonly imposing hardships on them.

(b) Description
The following is a passage of description:

> The offices of Messrs Snitchey and Craggs stood convenient, with an open door down two smooth steps, in the market-place; so that any angry farmer inclining towards hot water might tumble into it at once. Their special council-chamber and hall of conference was an old back room upstairs, with a low dark ceiling, which seemed to be knitting its brows gloomily in the consideration of tangled points of law. It was furnished with some high-backed leathern chairs, garnished with great goggle-eyed brass nails, of which, every here and there, two or three had fallen out – or had been picked out, perhaps, by the wandering thumbs and

forefingers of bewildered clients. There was a framed print of a great judge in it, every curl in whose dreadful wig had made a man's hair stand on end. Bales of papers filled the dusty closets, shelves and tables; and round the wainscot there were tiers of boxes, padlocked and fireproof, with people's names painted outside, which anxious visitors felt themselves, by a cruel enchantment, obliged to spell backwards and forwards, and to make anagrams of, while they sat, seeming to listen to Snitchey and Craggs, without comprehending one word of what they said. (Charles Dickens)

Comments

The special character of a description such as this is necessarily lost in a summary. The humorous comments (on the angry farmer, the ceiling, the brass nails, the judge's wig, the fireproof boxes) must be omitted, so that we are left with the dry bones that Dickens clothed with living flesh. In dealing with longer passages, the writer of a précis can often preserve something of the original effect.

Outline of précis

Position of offices – consulting-room – chairs – picture – papers – boxes.

Précis

The offices of Messrs Snitchey and Craggs were conveniently situated in the market-place. Clients were received in an old back room with a low dark ceiling. The furniture included some high-backed leather chairs ornamented with brass nails, some of which were missing. A framed print of a great judge adorned the wall. Bales of papers were to be seen everywhere, and round the wainscot were tiers of boxes, padlocked and fireproof, with names painted on them.

(c) Easy argument

In the summarizing of an argument, more care and skill are required than in dealing with narrative or description. An argument, of course, leads to a conclusion. This conclusion must be clearly perceived and clearly stated; and the stages by which it is reached must be plainly set out. In spite of the need for brevity in working, the connection of ideas must be preserved.

There were many obstacles to the development of commerce in the Middle Ages. Dangers by land and sea had to be considered by the merchant who wished to send his goods to some distant part; but as the towns grew and multiplied, the resolution and ingenuity of man rendered it possible for commerce to increase steadily, till by the dawn of the modern period every country in Western Europe had felt its beneficent influence. When we think of the poorness of communication, the vast forests, the inferior roads, the unbridged rivers, and the innumerable foes lining the trade routes, it would seem, at first sight, almost an impossibility for merchants in the north of Europe to have intercourse with those of the south. Then, again, the narrow spirit of the Middle Ages, the survival of feudalism, offered a difficulty which was almost as prohibitive to the transportation of merchandise as the robbers and pirates, noble and ignoble, who lay in wait for the trembling merchant. There was an elaborate system of dues and tolls which made most goods when they arrived safely at their destination a luxury beyond the means of the average man; and, furthermore, it was the practice for governments in those days to prohibit and prevent passage through their countries. Yet in spite of all difficulties the groups of towns which were developing in Northern and Southern Europe, and the manufacturing centres of the East and West, steadily increased their wealth and prosperity.

Outline of précis

Obstacles to commerce – (1) forests, roads, rivers, robbers, (2) survival of feudal system – dues and tolls; passage hindered – yet commerce developed.

Précis

There were many obstacles to the development of European commerce in the Middle Ages. There were vast forests, bad roads and unbridged rivers, and numerous bands of robbers were lying in wait for merchants. The feudal system still survived: an elaborate system of dues and tolls made goods too dear for most people; and, further, governments made a practice of hindering passage through their countries. Yet in spite of all these difficulties, commerce was carried on and developed, and the commercial centres steadily increased in wealth and prosperity.

(d) Short passages containing dialogue

The following is the method to be followed in the précis of dialogue:

(i) Read the passage through carefully in order to grasp the essentials of the situation, and take care to include only these in the précis. There is generally some clearly defined point in the dialogue. Arrange the material used in the précis so as to bring this out clearly.

(ii) Turn the direct speech of the original into indirect speech, so that the finished précis is a consecutive narrative in the third person and in the past tense.

The repetition of 'he said' is rarely necessary. Often several speeches can be run together, and some completely omitted. In the case of a question and a reply, it may be possible to give the question in narrative style and summarize the reply only in reported speech.

(iii) Pay due attention to proportion. Do not give so much space to the first part of the narrative that the remainder has to be crammed into a few words.

Mr Nupkins debated the matter within himself for a few seconds, and then, rising from his chair, and requesting Mr Pickwick and Sam to follow him, led the way into a small room which opened into the justice parlour. Desiring Mr Pickwick to walk to the farther end of the little apartment, and holding his hand upon the half-closed door, that he might be able to effect an immediate escape, in case there was the least tendency to a display of hostilities, Mr Nupkins expressed his willingness to hear the communication, whatever it might be.

'I will come to the point at once, Sir,' said Mr Pickwick, 'it affects yourself, and your credit, materially. I have every reason to believe, Sir, that you are harbouring in your house a gross impostor!'

'Two,' interrupted Sam, 'Mulberry agin all nature, for tears and willainy.'

'Sam,' said Mr Pickwick, 'if I am to render myself intelligible to this gentleman, I must beg you to control your feelings.'

'Werry sorry, Sir,' replied Mr Weller; 'but when I think o' that 'ere Job, I can't help opening the walve an inch or two.'

'In one word, Sir,' said Mr Pickwick, 'is my servant right in suspecting that a certain Captain Fitz-Marshall is in the habit of visiting here? Because,' added Mr Pickwick, as he saw that Mr Nupkins was about to offer a very indignant interruption – 'because, if he be, I know that person to be a –'

'Hush, hush,' said Mr Nupkins, closing the door. 'Know him to be what, Sir?'

'An unprincipled adventurer – a dishonourable character – a man who preys upon society, and makes easily-deceived people his dupes, Sir; his absurd, his foolish, his wretched dupes, Sir,' said the excited Mr Pickwick.

'Dear me,' said Mr Nupkins, colouring up very red, and altering his whole manner directly. 'Dear me, Mr –'

'Pickwick,' said Sam.

'Pickwick,' said the magistrate, 'dear me, Mr Pickwick, pray take a seat – you cannot mean this? Captain Fitz-Marshall!'

'Don't call him a cap'en,' said Sam, 'nor a Fitz-Marshall neither; he aint neither one nor t'other. He's a strolling actor, he is, and his name's Jingle; and if ever there was a wolf in a mulberry suit, that 'ere Job Trotter's him.'

'It is very true, Sir,' said Mr Pickwick, replying to the magistrate's look of amazement; 'my only business in this town is to expose the person of whom we now speak.'

And Mr Pickwick proceeded to pour into the horror-stricken ear of Mr Nupkins, an abridged account of all Mr Jingle's atrocities. He related how he had first met him, how he had eloped with Miss Wardle, how he had cheerfully resigned the lady for a pecuniary consideration, how he had entrapped him into a lady's boarding school at midnight, and how he (Mr Pickwick) now felt it his duty to expose his assumption of his present name and rank. (Charles Dickens)

Précis

Mr Nupkins nervously led Mr Pickwick and Sam Weller into a small adjoining room. Mr Pickwick bluntly told Mr Nupkins that he was harbouring an impostor. He explained – with assistance from Sam, who eagerly interrupted from time to time – that the Captain Fitz-Marshall who visited at the house was none other than the unprincipled adventurer Jingle. He gave the astonished Mr Nupkins a brief account of Jingle's previous disgraceful exploits, and expressed his determination to expose him.

Comment

Note how Sam Weller's frequent remarks are rendered in the précis as '. . .with assistance from Sam who eagerly interrupted from time to time'.

(e) Fiction in general

Every work of fiction is more than a mere narrative of facts or account of conversations: it has a particular point – an underlying idea illustrated by the events or the dialogue. This central idea of the story must be clearly brought out in the summary. It is not enough to state baldly the facts narrated by the story-teller: the significance of what has been written must be made clear.

Correspondence

A letter, whether dealing with a personal or business topic, is a kind of essay and thus is subject to the ordinary rules of composition; but as a form of writing it has certain characteristics that must receive special attention. In business correspondence it is customary to observe set forms, but in letters to friends these forms are generally dispensed with. It will therefore be convenient to deal separately with personal letters, business letters and general business correspondence.

133. PERSONAL LETTERS

Whereas in an essay the writer talks, so to speak, to the world at large, in a personal letter the writer usually has only one reader in mind, and s/he can, therefore, adopt a much more free and intimate style. The ostensible subject of the writer's communication may be a holiday, or his/her experiences in a new post, but the real aim must be to set up a current of sympathetic feeling between writer and acquaintance. The best letter, therefore, resembles a conversation on paper; it makes the recipient feel that s/he is actually chatting to the letter-writer.

It is obviously impossible to lay down any absolute rules about how letters should be written. Letter-writing, like any other form of composition, is an individual matter, dependent largely upon personal tastes and peculiarities. The style of a personal letter will, of course, be much more familiar than that of other types of composition. In real life it is often full of slang and colloquialism, a linguistic style which is usually best avoided in formal or public writing.

Although a personal letter should be without formality, it should not be formless. The ideas should be given proper sequence and should be arranged in suitable paragraphs.

(a) The form of a personal letter
It is not essential for a familiar letter to follow a stereotyped form: very intimate friends, in fact, often vary or omit altogether some of the points mentioned below. However, the following are useful guidelines to bear in mind.

(i) The heading. The address from which the letter is being written, together with the date, is placed at the top right-hand corner of the first sheet.

(ii) The salutation. This comes on the left-hand, a little below the date. It varies according to the degree of intimacy between the correspondents. The usual forms are 'Dear John' or 'My Dear John'.

(iii) The body of the letter.

(iv) The subscription and signature. The usual forms of subscription are: between friends – yours sincerely; between relatives – yours affectionately, your loving daughter, your affectionate nephew etc.

(b) Other private letters
There are other types of personal letters that are more formal in tone than those we have discussed above – for example a letter for publication in a newspaper, a letter to some public official regarding the service under his or her control, a letter to a local councillor, or a letter to a Member of Parliament. Such letters take the following form:

(i) Letter heading. The address of the writer and the date, as in personal letters.

(ii) Name and address of addressee. This may be placed on the left-hand side of the page, a line below the date, or it may be placed on the left-hand side of the page at the foot of the letter.

(iii) The salutation. This is placed beneath the name and address of the addressee, or, where that name and address is appended at the foot of the letter, the salutation appears a line below the date, on the left-hand side of the page. The salutation is usually 'Dear Sir/Madam', but 'Sir' can be employed in letters to newspapers.

(iv) The body of the letter. This will, of course, depend on the subject of the letter, but whatever has to be said should be said as concisely as possible. Newspapers have a limited amount of space to devote to correspondence from readers.

134. BUSINESS LETTERS

The rules of grammar and of style considered elsewhere in this book must be applied in the writing of business correspondence just as much as in any other field of English composition. Good grammar and the correct construction of sentences are as essential in a business letter as they are in an essay; but all too frequently these matters are overlooked, since a letter conveys to the recipient an impression of the business personality of the writer and the firm represented.

Although it is difficult to formulate any precise definition of what is and what is not recognized as good style in the writing of business letters and reports, there are, nevertheless, certain rules that must not be disregarded. An attempt will be made in the following paragraphs to deal with each of these in turn, and also to indicate those matters of form and arrangement that must be adhered to by anyone who wishes to write a good business letter.

The form of a business letter
The letter usually consists of the following divisions:

Letter heading
Name and address of addressee
Salutation
Introductory paragraph
Body of the letter
Closing paragraph
Subscription and signature

(i) The letter heading
This will set forth the name of the firm, its postal and fax address, its telephone number and fax number, and the nature of its business. The heading is usually printed.

Limited companies must be careful to add the word 'Limited' (or Ltd) or PLC to their names, and to give the address of the registered office. Private firms must specify on their writing paper the names of the partners. If a letter emanates from a special department, for example the Secretary's office, Personnel Department, Accounts, Business Manager's Department, Post Room, the Registrar's Department etc., an indication of the fact will be given, together with the separate address, if any. Branch offices of a large firm usually specify the address of the principal or head office. Frequently, an indication is given that replies should be addressed to the issuing company and not to individuals.

In the heading, room is usually left for the date of dispatch of the letter and for a reference number, which should be quoted in the reply and in any subsequent correspondence between the same parties. The date should give the number of the day, the name of the month and the number of the year, in that order. 25th May

1991 is better than May 25th, 1991. It is better to avoid abbreviation and to write the name of the month in full. On no account should a letter be dated simply 'Tuesday', for this will give no indication of the exact date of sending. Some letter-writers adopt the practice of giving numbers alone in dates, e.g. 25/5/91 or 25.5.91, but this is regarded as lazy by others. It is worth remembering that Americans and continental Europeans use the number system differently from the British. Typically the date would be rendered as 5.25.91.

(ii) Name and address of addressee

The letter must always begin with the name and full address of the person to whom it is directed. This appears close to the left-hand margin, and usually occupies two or three lines. Each successive line may be further indented, thus:

Messrs Rowland and Ward,
  5 Castle Street,
    Liverpool.

Or each line may be ranged left, thus:

The Acme Roofing Company,
16 Hall Lane,
London EC3.

The second of these is neater and now more widespread. When letters are dispatched in 'window' envelopes, the addressee's details which are printed on to the letter itself must also function as the address label. It is also advisable to insert details on any continuation sheets that may be used. These precautions will enable a clear record to be retained on the carbon copy or photocopy.

It was once the practice to address all male addressees as 'Esquire' (or 'Esq.') but this is ornate and overformal and now the prefix 'Mr' will suffice. If the addressee is female and her marital status is unknown, or if she feels her marital status is not significant to the correspondence, then the prefix 'Ms' should be used.

Partnerships usually take the designation 'Messrs', although this is omitted where the firm-name begins with a title, e.g. Sir John Watson and Sons, or where the name is impersonal, e.g. The Palmer Tyre Co. 'Messrs' must never be used where the name is impersonal, e.g. The Midland Bank, or Imperial Chemical Industries PLC.

In writing to limited companies, local authorities, professional societies, charitable institutions etc., it is usual to address a particular official such as the secretary or general manager.

All letters should bear the post code, on a separate line.

Threadneedle Street
London
EC2R 4SC

The following are examples of addresses illustrating the foregoing rules:

Dr Henry Brown
17 Rodney Street
Liverpool
L2 4ER

Messrs Start and Co.
51-55 Stevenson Square
Manchester
M4 8PQ

The Palgrave Ironworks Co. Ltd
20 Wilton Street
Oxford
OX2 5GU

(iii) The salutation
This comes beneath the recipient's address, close to the left-hand margin.

The salutation 'Sir' may be used for all Government correspondence, very formal business letters, and some letters to newspaper editors. It is, however, somewhat pompous for general use.

'Dear Sir' is the most widely-used salutation in commercial correspondence, and the equivalent for a female recipient is 'Dear Madam'. If the gender of the recipient is unknown, then the option 'Dear Sir/Madam' should be employed.

'Dear Mr Jones' is somewhat more familiar than 'Dear Sir' and may be used intentionally to convey a personal touch, or where the addressee has intimate or frequent business relations with the writer. For example, letters to agents and representatives, or to clients with whom one is socially acquainted, might well begin with 'Dear Mr – '. Great care is necessary, however. The phrase should not be used without a real reason, and it is best avoided if the writer has the slightest suspicion that it is unwelcome. For example, if replies from the addressee invariably begin with 'Dear Sir', then a return to the more formal mode of address would appear desirable!

The salutation 'Gentlemen' is not widely used in ordinary business correspondence, but is often used for letters and reports addressed by an employee to his/her board of directors, and in letters or reports addressed to a committee, public body or local authority. It is a more dignified mode of salutation than the usual 'Dear Sirs', and should be used whenever the writer wishes to show respect for the addressees. The form 'Gents.' should never be employed!

To avoid the sexist implications of the above form, one might reasonably channel one's address to an official body via 'Chair' or 'Chairperson'.

(iv) Personal titles
Special forms of address are necessary for persons in high office and those who carry titles or rank. The following are examples of the correct usage:

Royal Duke: to be announced or referred to as 'His Royal Highness the Duke of York'. Salutation, 'Sir', or more formally, 'May it please your Royal Highness'.

Duke: to be announced or referred to as 'His Grace, the Duke of Bedford'. Salutation, 'My Lord Duke' or 'Your Grace'.

Marquess: to be announced or referred to as 'The Most Honourable the Marquess of Bute'. Salutation, 'My Lord Marquess'.

Earl: to be announced or referred to as 'The Right Honourable, the Earl of Coventry'. Salutation, 'My Lord'.

Viscount: to be announced or referred to as 'The Right Honourable the Viscount Cowdray'. Salutation, 'My Lord'.

Baron: to be announced or referred to as 'The Right Honourable Lord Airedale'. Salutation, 'My Lord'.

Baronet: to be announced or referred to as 'Sir George Chesterton, Bart.'. Salutation, 'Sir'.

Knight: to be announced or referred to as 'Sir Hall Crescent'. Salutation, 'Sir'.

(v) Titles of offices
Archbishop: to be announced or referred to as 'The Most Revd His Grace the Lord Archbishop of Canterbury'. Salutation, 'Your Grace' or 'My Lord Archbishop'.

Bishop: to be announced or referred to as 'The Right Revd the Lord Bishop of Ely'. Salutation, 'My Lord'.

Dean: to be announced or referred to as 'The Very Revd Dean of St Albans'. Salutation, 'Mr Dean' or 'Reverend Sir'.

Clergyman: to be announced or referred to as 'Revd T. Wardale'. Salutation 'Reverend Sir'.

Lord Chief Justice: To be announced or referred to as 'The Rt. Hon. the Lord Chief Justice'. Salutation, 'My Lord'.

Judge: to be announced or referred to as 'The Honourable Mr Justice Romer'. Salutation, 'Sir'.

Member of the Privy Council: to be announced or referred to as 'The Rt. Hon. Gerald Gordon, PC'. Salutation, 'Sir'.

Lord Mayor: to be announced or referred to as 'The Rt. Hon. the Lord Mayor of London'. Salutation, 'My Lord' or 'My Lord Mayor'.

Lord Provost: to be announced or referred to as 'The Rt. Hon. the Lord Provost of Edinburgh'. Salutation, 'My Lord' or 'My Lord Provost'.

Mayor: to be announced or referred to as 'The Worshipful the Mayor of Cromer'. Salutation, 'Sir' or 'Madam'.

Alderman: to be announced or referred to as 'Mr Alderman Green'.

Councillor: to be announced or referred to as 'Mr/Mrs/Ms Councillor Brown'.

(vi) The introductory paragraph

The introductory paragraph of a letter, as its name implies, serves to introduce the matters with which the letter deals. In replies, the introductory paragraph will contain a reference to previous correspondence, and will thus enable the recipient to recall the matters dealt with and facilitate the work of looking up earlier letters. Thus, a letter beginning 'In reply to your letter AF/M of the 5th January . . .' or 'Following on my letter of the 7th March . . .', will enable instant reference to the correspondence in question, and, by easing the work of the addressee, will help to secure goodwill.

A practice frequently adopted is to head the letter, immediately after the salutation, with a few words indicative of its subject or contents. Sometimes the heading begins with the word 're', but strictly, this word should be confined to legal matters and is better avoided in an ordinary business letter. For example:

Re: Lancaster House Farm.

Staff Insurance Fund.

Contract 1760-40 Cane-backed Chairs.

(vii) The body of the letter

The contents of the body of the letter will, of course, depend upon the particular circumstances, but it is nevertheless possible to give a few rules that will apply to every business letter.

Where the letter is short and deals with only one fact or item, one paragraph is usually sufficient; if several matters are mentioned, however, each should be dealt with in a separate paragraph or paragraphs, according to the length of each discussion. If the letter consists of several paragraphs, they must be arranged in logical order, with a view to presenting the facts in the clearest possible way.

A well-paragraphed letter is easier to read than one which is merely a solid mass of handwriting or typewriting.

(viii) The closing paragraph

Very frequently, particularly in sales letters, the whole of the argument is summed up in a final paragraph, and consequently this should be as forceful and convincing as possible. In an ordinary letter, the closing paragraph may consist simply of one or two phrases of courteous form, expressing a hope for a favourable reply, or assuring the addressee of every attention. Many of these phrases have become stereotyped, and should be avoided. The following are examples of these stereotypes:

Assuring you of our best attention at all times,

Thanking you in anticipation of a favourable reply,

(ix) The subscription and signature

The subscription of a business letter is almost invariably one of four or five phrases; the choice will depend upon the custom of the firm on behalf of which the letter is written, and also upon the degree of intimacy existing between the writer and the recipient. The rules laid down for the salutation apply equally to the subscription, and the two must always agree, not only in number and wording, but also in style.

'Yours faithfully' is the subscription most frequently used. Like 'Dear Sir', it is neither too formal nor too casual, and it is suitable for practically all occasions. The subscription 'Yours sincerely' is usually avoided when a letter has begun with the formal salutation 'Dear Sir' or 'Dear Madam'. If the name of the recipient is unknown or has not been used, then 'Yours faithfully' is more apt. 'Yours truly' is less commonly used, perhaps because it is somewhat colourless.

'Yours obediently' and 'Your obedient servant' are not very usual today although they are sometimes used in official correspondence and (quite incorrectly) by applicants for jobs.

The signature should always be in the same form so as to be instantly recognizable, and should be written by hand. It is a common practice for the name of the writer to be typewritten under the signature. The firm-name may be typescript, or may be imprinted on the letter with a rubber stamp, but the name of a responsible official should always be signed below, as indicated in the following example:

The Huntingtower Co. Ltd
Walter Stead
Managing Director.

Letters may be written in either the first person singular or the first person plural; i.e. either 'I' or 'we' may be used. Different firms take different views, but it may be said that the first person singular is better when the correspondent is the owner of the business or is merely voicing his personal opinions or the opinions of a department, and that the first person plural is desirable when the letter is expressing the views of the firm as a whole. 'We' carries somewhat more weight than 'I', however, and should always be used where it is not obviously unsuitable.

It is, of course, essential that the number of the person used should be the same throughout the letter, and that it should correspond with the signature. A letter written in the first person singular must be signed by an individual, while a letter written in the first person plural must bear the signature of a firm or company. Where a correspondent is writing a letter on behalf of a firm, there is, of course, no objection to the use of the first person singular as a general rule and the first person plural when wishing to give the opinion or decision of the firm as a whole.

(x) 'Per Pro.' signatures

In a large firm it is obviously impossible for the head of the business to deal with all the correspondence, and certain employees are therefore authorized to sign for firms; they are then said to sign 'per procurationem', or 'per pro.'. The authority may result from custom (as with a secretary to a limited company), or from the execution of a proper Power of Attorney. Unless the authority exists in some form or another, the signature should be 'For Smith and Co., Gordon Craig'. The existence of a proper authorization should always be indicated by the signature, for example:

per pro. Kenworthy Limited,
John Green.

or

pp. Laura Hardman
Sales Executive

In modern practice, however, 'per pro.' is frequently omitted, and the words descriptive of the office held by the signatory, e.g. Secretary, Sales Manager etc., are usually added. The recipient is then in a much better position to estimate the exact scope of the powers and responsibilities of the correspondent.

135. THE ESSENTIALS OF A GOOD LETTER

(a) Knowing what to say
Obviously a really good letter cannot be written unless the writer knows exactly what s/he wishes to convey to his/her correspondent. Hence the first essential is to obtain a grasp of all the necessary facts and to arrange them logically and systematically. Writing, like speaking, involves the expression of one's thoughts accurately and with clarity; and any confusion of ideas leads inevitably to confusion of expression.

(b) Clearness
Nothing pleases the recipient of a business letter more than to read a series of clear-cut, unambiguous sentences. At one reading s/he can take in all that is essential, and his/her time is not wasted with unimportant items.

(c) Conciseness or brevity
Every business letter should be as concise as the subject matter will permit. People who receive many letters every day cannot afford to devote more than a minute or two to reading and mastering the contents of each one. Brevity is, therefore, absolutely essential, and may be considered from two standpoints.

Firstly, what need not be said should be entirely omitted. A business letter must stick to the point, all irrelevancies being ruthlessly discarded, however interesting they may seem to the writer.

Secondly, what must be said should be expressed in the most concise form compatible with the laws of grammar and courtesy. The faults of redundancy have been dealt with in an earlier chapter (pp.63-4); in letters, especially, avoid such expressions as 'we are both agreed', 'our entire monopoly', 'closely united together' etc., where tautology is present. Further, do not use extravagant expressions of pleasure, sorrow etc., such as 'exceedingly glad', 'wonderfully good', 'immensely popular' etc. when the simple adverb 'very' can be used with equal force and less artificial ornament.

(d) Accuracy of statement
The statements in a business letter or document should be as accurate as it is within the power and information of the writer to make them. Accuracy depends largely on a thorough knowledge of the subject-matter; inaccurate and inconsistent statements only too frequently arise from an incomplete knowledge of facts and circumstances.

(e) Courteous phrasing
Courtesy is a necessary attribute of the good business letter. A business letter can and must be courteous, whatever the occasion. Even a final demand for payment of an overdue account can be written in a pleasant style.

At the same time, it is essential to guard against servility. A cringing attitude merely invites a blow.

It may usefully be added that everything tends to look worse in 'black and white'. In a discussion, a suggestion may be greeted by 'Oh, but that's idiotic! I couldn't possibly agree', accompanied by a friendly laugh. In a letter, the cheerfulness is missing, the personal touch is absent, and the true implications of the remark are misjudged.

(f) Commercial English

Until quite recently most business letters were couched in a meaningless jargon known as 'business English'. Inherited from the early Victorian period, business English was a peculiar mass of conventions that were neither sensible nor convincing, and merely served to leave in the mind of the reader an unpleasant feeling of servility.

According to business English a letter is never referred to simply as a letter. Thus the third letter of a series would begin, 'With reference to your esteemed favour of the 5th and our respects of the 7th inst.' Every letter was an 'esteemed favour' from the recipient's point of view, whether it contained a cheque or large consignment, or was alleging short order.

Similarly, every letter sent out was 'our respects', the term being applied to final demands for payment as well as letters of congratulation. The correct designation for the firm to whom the letter was addressed was always 'your goodselves'; the fact that no dictionary contains the word 'goodselves' was either unknown or ignored.

The natural result of the continued misuse of such phrases was that they lost what little significance they ever possessed; moreover any letter containing them appeared machine-made and processed. Gradually objections to business English became articulate, and many of the more progressive firms began to throw overboard the stock phrases that made every letter seem alike, and to substitute accessible, frank and clear-cut English.

This movement was greatly accelerated by the increasing Americanization of the business world. As English became the language of international business and diplomacy, the need for an unambiguous language increased, which is, thankfully, what we have now.

136. FAXES

Much business correspondence is now conducted by fax. There is no strict rule for the sending of faxes but it is usual to use a covering sheet with information such as the fax numbers of both the recipient and the sender.
A typical layout for a fax would be as follows:

> FAX TRANSMISSION
> FROM: STEVE RODGERS, TOP PRODUCTIONS
> TO: PETER HART, BETTER DESIGN
> RE: DOCKLAND DESIGN PROJECT
> DATE: 6.07.90

We have received the information for the new colour scheme, and will return our plans by fax or courier today.
Yours sincerely,
Steve.

137. CVs AND COVERING LETTERS

(a) The general format of a curriculum vitae covers the following:

(1) Personal details
(2) Education and qualifications
(3) Experience and details of career history
(4) Personal interests, hobbies and pastimes
(5) Other details.

Brevity is essential in CV-writing. The person who is screening the applications will want to be able to find the details easily and in a form uncluttered by irrelevant details. You may well be able to write several pages on your virtues in your first post, but a potential employer will be interested in an informed synopsis. Unless you have large amounts of exceptionally relevant experience it is essential to keep the CV on one side of a sheet of A4 paper.

(b) You should always send a covering letter with a curriculum vitae and application form. If your letter is unsolicited and speculative, this is even more important.

Your letter can be typed or handwritten as long as the end result is clear. The letter must be neat – many applications have been turned down because the recruiter was unable to read the contents.

Any letter that you send in connection with gaining employment must be formal. It must be set out properly and show respect to the person you are writing to. Remember that if you start the letter by saying 'Dear Sir' you must end with 'Yours faithfully', and that if you use the person's name, as in 'Dear Mrs Ryder', you should end with 'Yours sincerely'. Note that both the 'f' of faithfully and the 's' of sincerely are in lower case and should not be given capital letters.

Spend some time composing your letter and avoid clichés. The letter is important as this will be read before the CV itself. It therefore creates the first impression and sets the tone of the application. It must contain all the salient points which are not included in the CV but are pertinent to this particular application. You may wish to draw attention to certain factors within the CV which apply to the post you are interested in.

You should avoid phrases like 'I can communicate effectively at all levels.' This, like the phrase 'I have initiative . . .', is virtually impossible to prove without added detail, which takes up space. If you have initiative or can communicate effectively at all levels, make sure that this is evident from the information in your CV.

You should avoid phrases like these if the advertisement asks for this kind of quality. Other applicants will doubtless be stating that they have great initiative or whatever in their applications too, and that would mean that your application would look exactly like all the others.

Appendix 1

A glossary of grammatical terms

Accidence That part of grammar which deals with the inflexion (i.e. the accidents) of words.

Adjective A word which describes, telling us what something or someone is like, e.g. the *big* man, an *exciting* trip, an *evil* act.

Adverb A word which qualifies a verb. An adverb indicates how, when, where and in what manner actions are performed. Adverbs can also qualify adjectives or other adverbs, e.g. a *very* beautiful view; she worked *exceedingly* hard.

Apposition The placing together of two words, especially two nouns, one being a complement to the other and following without any conjunction, e.g. Mrs Gupta, *the manager*, called me in.

Archaism A word or phrase that is old-fashioned or obsolete, e.g. methinks, stenography, to wit.

Auxiliary A term applied to verbs used in the conjugation of other verbs, e.g. I *have* paid the bill; we *will* go to Leeds.

Clause A group of words containing at least a verb and a subject, but not necessarily forming a complete sentence.

Collective A collective noun is one which is singular in form but which names a group of people or things, e.g. flock, swarm, lorryload.

Comparative Adjectives and adverbs are used in the comparative mode when they place persons, places and actions in contrast with each other. More than . . ., greater than . . ., as good as . . ., are all phrases used to introduce a comparison.

Compound Tenses made up of more than one element are called compound tenses. These are made by using auxiliary verbs, or present or past participles, e.g. she was dancing; I have thought.

Conjugation The conjugation of a verb is the inflexion for person, number, tense, voice, mood etc.

Conjunction A word connecting sentences or clauses, or coordinating words in the same clause, e.g. and, or, while, but.

Consonant A sound which is combined with a vowel in order to make a syllable.

Definite article *The* is the definite article.

Demonstrative A class of words used to indicate, for emphasis or clarity, the particular referent or referents intended, e.g. this, that, these, those.

Determiner A word that limits or modifies a noun, e.g. that, my, his.

Diphthong A combination of two vowel sounds forming one syllable, e.g. the middle sound in h*ou*se. Diphthong also describes composite vowels, such as *ae* in C*ae*sar.

Etymology The history of the origin and modification of a particular word in a language.

Gerund A verbal noun which ends in -ing, when used as part of the verb, e.g. *learning* is fun; she grew impatient with *waiting*.

Hybrid word A word whose parts have been derived from two different languages, e.g. officialdom, where *official* comes from Latin and *-dom* from Old English.

Imperative The mood of a verb used for commands, e.g. walk! don't run!

Indefinite article *A* (or *an*) is the indefinite article.

Inflexion (inflection) An inflexion is a change in form undergone by a word in accordance with a change in its meaning or relationship to other words in the sentence, e.g. boy, boy's, boys'; man, men; sleep, slept; he, his, him; who, whom, whose.

Interjection A word which expresses a feeling as an exclamation and which is differentiated as a separate part of speech, e.g. Oh! Ah!

Interrogative A word or phrase which denotes a question, e.g. why? what for? in which way?

Mood A verb-form expressing the manner in which the act, event or fact is conceived, whether as actual, contingent, possible, desirable etc.

Morphology The science of the forms of words in a language; (especially) the consistent patterns of inflexion, combination, derivation and change that may be observed and classified.

Noun A word used as the name of anything, be it of people, places, objects or abstractions, e.g. David, Newcastle, video, love.

Orthography The part of grammar which deals with letters and spelling; correct spelling.

Parts of speech Words are said to belong to one of eight categories according to the function they perform in a sentence. Hence, words may be nouns, pronouns, verbs, adjectives, adverbs, prepositions, conjunctions or interjections.

Phonetics The study of speech-sounds.

Preposition A word or group of words used to relate the noun or pronoun it is placed in front of, to other constituent parts of a sentence, e.g. with, in, at, to.

Pronoun A word used in place of a noun to denote a person or a thing which has already been mentioned or implied, e.g. she, it, they.

(to) Qualify To modify, limit or narrow the scope, force etc. of a statement, opinion or word.

Referent The object or idea to which a word or phrase refers.

Sentence A series of words, containing a subject, predicate etc., which expresses a complete thought. When written, a sentence is introduced with a capital letter and is end-stopped (with a full point or question/exclamation mark).

Syllable A sound forming a word or part of a word, containing one vowel sound, with or without a consonant or consonants, and uttered at a single effort or vocal impulse, e.g. *e/col/o/gy* has 4 syllables.

Syntax A branch of grammar which deals with the relationship of words when they are used in sentences.

Tense A form taken by a verb to indicate the time, and also the continuance or completedness of an action.

Verb Perennially described as a 'doing word', but truly a word which describes an action, e.g. to run, to fight, to talk; or a state, e.g. to be, to have, to hope.

Vowel A sound able to make a syllable or to be sounded alone. Vowel-sounds are expressed in English by the letters a, e, i, o, u, (y), and by symbols or groups of letters, e.g. *au* in *au*ght, *ou* in n*ou*ght, *ie* in bel*ie*ve.

Appendix 2

Common prefixes and suffixes

PREFIXES

a-, an- not, without *asexual*.
aero- aircraft *aerodrome*; air *aerobic*.
agro- agriculture *agrobiology*.
ambi- two, both *ambidextrous*.
Anglo- English, British *Anglo-French*.
ante- before *antenatal*.
anthropo- human being *anthropology*.
anti- against, opposite, opposing *anti-establishment*.
arch- chief, highest *archbishop*.
astro- star *astrophysics*.
audio- sound, hearing *audiovisual*.
auto- self, oneself *autobiography*; automatic *autopilot*; automotive, automobile *autocross*.
bi- two, twice *bicycle*.
biblio- book *bibliophile*.
bio- life, living material *biology*.
by(e)- secondary *by-product*.
cardi(o)- heart *cardiovascular*.
centi- hundred *centipede*; hundredth part *centimetre*.
chron(o)- time *chronology*.
circum- round *circumnavigate*.
co- together *cooperate*.
con-, col-, com-, cor- with, together *conjoin*.
contra- against *contraception*.
counter- against, opposite *counter-clockwise*; matching *counterpart*.
crypto- secret, hidden *cryptofascist*.
cyclo- circle *cyclorama*.
de- to do the opposite *decentralize*; to remove *deseed*; to make less *devalue*.
deca- ten *decathlon*.
deci- tenth part *decilitre*.
demi- half, part *demigod*.
derm- skin *dermatitis*.
di- two, double *dioxide*.
dis- opposite, not *dishonest*; to remove *dismember*.
electro- electricity, electrical *electromagnetic*.

en-, em- to cause to be *enlarge*; to put in or on *endanger*.
equi- equal *equidistant*.
Eur(o)- European *Eurasian*; European Economic Community *Eurocurrency*.
ex- former *ex-president*.
extra- beyond, outside *extraterrestrial*.
fore- before *foretell*; front, front part *foreleg*.
geo- earth *geography*.
gyn(o)-, gynaec(o)- female, woman *gynaecology*.
haem(o)- blood *haemorrhage*.
hemi- half *hemisphere*.
hetero- different, other *heterosexual*.
hex(a)- six *hexagram*.
hol(o)- complete, whole *holistic*.
homo- same, alike *homogeneous*.
hydro- water *hydroelectric*; hydrogen *hydrochloric*.
hyper- more than normal, excessive *hyperactive*.
hypo- less than normal, low, too low *hypothermia*.
in-, il-, im-, ir- not *insensitive*.
infra- below, beneath *infrared*.
inter- between *intercity*.
intra- in, within *intravenous*.
iso- equal, uniform, the same *isobar*.
kilo- thousand *kilogram*.
macro- large, large-scale *macroclimate*.
mal- bad, badly *malnutrition*.
matri- mother *matriarch*.
mega- million *megaton*; large, extremely large *megastar*.
micro- small, small-scale *microcomputer*.
milli- thousandth part *millilitre*.
mini- small *mini-skirt*.
mis- bad, badly *misbehave*; not *mistrust*.
mono- single, one *monoplane*.

multi- many, several *multiracial*.
neo- new, recent *neo-Georgian*.
neuro- nerve, nervous system *neuroscience*.
non- not *nonsmoker*.
oct-, octa-, octo- eight *octopus*.
omni- all *omnivore*.
osteo- bone *osteoarthritis*.
out- beyond, exceeding, surpassing *outlive*; fourth *outpouring*; outside, external *outlying*.
over- above *overlord*; outer *overcoat*; to much *overeat*.
paed(o)- child, *paediatrician*.
palaeo- old, archaic, early *Palaeolithic*.
pan- all *pan-American*.
para- beside *parallel*; beyond *paranormal*; abnormal *paranoia*; resembling *paratyphoid*; associated, supplementary *paramedical*.
patri- father *patriarch*.
pent(a)- five *pentagon*.
photo- light *photosensitive*; photography *photocopy*.
physi(o)- nature, living things *physiology*; physical *physiotherapy*.
poly- many *polyglot*.
post- after *postdate*.
pre- before *prehistoric*.
pro- favouring *pro-American*; substitute for *pro-consul*.
prot(o)- first, original *prototype*.
pseud(o)- false *pseudonym*.
psych(o)- mind *psychoanalysis*.
quadr(i)- four *quadruped*.
quasi- partly, seemingly *quasi-judicial*.
radio- radiation *radiology*; radioactive, radioactivity *radioisotope*.
re- again *rewrite*.
retro- back, backwards *retrogress*.
self- oneself, itself *self-discipline*.
semi- half *semicircle*; partly *semi-conscious*.
socio- social, society *sociology*.
step- related by remarriage *stepsister*.
sub- below, under *subsoil*; less than, incompletely *subhuman*; subordinate, subdivision *subcontinent*.
super- above, greater, exceeding, more, superior *superpower*.
syn-, sym- together, with *synthesis*.
techno- technology, technical *technocracy*.

tele- over a distance *telecommunications*.
tetra- four *tetrahedron*.
theo- gods, God *theology*.
thermo- heat *thermometer*.
trans- across *transatlantic*.
tri- three *triangle*.
ultra- above, beyond *ultraviolet*.
un- not *unhappy*; to do the opposite *unknot*.
under- below, underneath *underpass*; insufficient *underfunding*; less important *undersecretary*.
uni- one *unicycle*.
vice- one next below *vice-president*.

SUFFIXES

-able, -ible that can be *washable*; having the quality of *comfortable*. **-ability, -ibility.**
-ade fruit drink *lemonade*.
-aholic, -oholic (one) addicted to *workaholic*.
-ana, -iana objects etc. belonging to *Victoriana*.
-arch ruler, leader, governor *monarch*. **-archy.**
-arian believer in, supporter of *vegetarian*; one connected with *librarian*.
-athon, -thon large-scale contest or event *telethon*.
-cide killing, killer *fungicide*. **-cidal.**
-cracy government, rule *democracy*; dominant or ruling class *aristocracy*.
-crat supporter of (the type of government) *democrat*; member of (a dominant class) *aristocrat*. **-cratic.**
-dom state or condition of being *boredom*; realm, domain *kingdom*.
-ectomy surgical removal *mastectomy*.
-ee one to whom something is done *payee*; one who is *absentee*; small version of *bootee*.
-eer one engaged in *profiteer*.
-er one who or that which does or is *employer*; one engaged in *lawyer*; one coming from *Londoner*.
-ese (people or language) of or from *Chinese*; language associated with *journalese*.
-esque in the style of *statuesque*.

-ess female *lioness*.

-ette small version of *kitchenette*; female *majorette*; imitation *satinette*.

-fold times *two-fold*.

-form having the form of *cruciform*.

-free without *lead-free*.

-friendly helpful to, supporting *user-friendly*.

-ful amount that fills something *bucketful*; full of *colourful*; having or causing *peaceful*.

-fy another form of **-ify.**

-gram drawn or written record *cardiogram*; message, greeting *kissogram*.

-graph instrument that records *seismograph*; something recorded or represented *autograph*. **-graphic, -graphy.**

-hood time or condition of being *childhood*.

-iana another form of **-ana.**

-ible, -ibility another form of **-able, -ability.**

-ics science, study *electronics*.

-ify to make or become *purify*; to fill with *terrify*.

-ise another form of **-ize.**

-ish like, similar to *childish*; somewhat *baldish*.

-ism state, condition *heroism*; doctrine, movement, system, theory *Buddhism*; discrimination on grounds of *racism*.

-ist follower or practitioner of a doctrine, science etc. *botanist*.

-ite (person) of or from, or that adheres to or supports *Israelite*; mineral *calcite*.

-itis disease *bronchitis*.

-ize, -ise to make or become *neutralize*.

-kin small version of *lambkin*.

-latry worship *idolatry*.

-less without *harmless*.

-let small version of *piglet*.

-like resembling *ladylike*.

-ling small, young or lesser version of *duckling*.

-logy science, theory *biology*; writing, treatise *trilogy*. **-logical, -logist.**

-meter instrument for measuring *barometer*.

-monger dealer in *fishmonger*.

-nik one connected with *beatnik*.

-oholic another form of **-aholic.**

-oid like, resembling *planetoid*.

-ology, -ological, -ologist another form of **-logy.**

-or another form of **-er.**

-osis action, process *metamorphosis*; diseased condition *thrombosis*.

-ped foot *quadruped*. **-pedal.**

-phile, -phil lover of *Anglophile*. **-philia** love of, attraction or tendency towards *necrophilia*. **-philiac.**

-phobe one who hates or fears *xenophobe*. **-phobia** hatred or fear of *claustrophobia*. **-phobic.**

-phone speaker of (a language) *Francophone*; sound *xylophone*.

-proof resisting, protecting against *heatproof*.

-scape view, scene *landscape*.

-scope instrument for viewing *microscope*. **-scopy.**

-ship condition, state, position *membership*; skill *craftsmanship*.

-some characterized by, full of *troublesome*; group of so many *foursome*.

-speak language, jargon *computerspeak*.

-thon another form of **-athon.**

-tomy surgical incision *lobotomy*.

-ward, -wards towards *upward*.

-ware articles *silverware*.

-ways in the direction, manner or position of *sideways*.

-wise in the direction, manner or position of *clockwise*; concerning *money-wise*.

-y having, full of, covered with *dirty*; inclined to *sleepy*; like *wintry*; affectionate term used esp. with children *doggy*.

Appendix 3

English irregular verbs

Infinitive	Past Tense	Past Participle
abide	abode	abode
arise	arose	arisen
awake	awoke	awoke *or* awaked
be *Pres. Indic.* am is are	was were	been
bear	bore	borne *or* born
beat	beat	beaten
become	became	become
befall	befell	befallen
beget	begot	begotten
begin	began	begun
behold	beheld	beheld
bend	bent	bent *or* bended (*rare*)
bereave	bereaved *or* bereft	bereaved *or* bereft
beseech	besought	besought
bestride	bestrode	bestridden
bid	bade	bidden
bide	bode *or* bided	bided
bind	bound	bound
bite	bit	bitten
bleed	bled	bled
blow	blew	blown
break	broke	broken
breed	bred	bred
bring	brought	brought
build	built	built
burn	burnt *or* burned	burnt *or* burned
burst	burst	burst
buy	bought	bought
Pres. Indic. can	could	–
cast	cast	cast
catch	caught	caught
chide	chid	chidden
choose	chose	chosen
cleave (*v.t.* to split)	cleft	cleft *or* cloven
cleave (*v.i.* to cling)	cleaved	cleaved
cling	clung	clung
clothe	clothed	clothed *or* clad
come	came	come
cost	cost	cost
creep	crept	crept
crow	crowed *or* crew	crowded
cut	cut	cut
deal	dealt	dealt

Infinitive	Past Tense	Past Participle
dig	dug	dug
do	did	done
draw	drew	drawn
dream	dreamt *or* dreamed	dreamt *or* dreamed
drink	drank	drunk
drive	drove	driven
dwell	dwelt	dwelt
eat	ate	eaten
fall	fell	fallen
feed	fed	fed
feel	felt	felt
fight	fought	fought
find	found	found
flee	fled	fled
fling	flung	flung
fly	flew	flown
forbear	forbore	forborne
forbid	forbade *or* forbad	forbidden
foresee	foresaw	foreseen
forget	forgot	forgotten *or* forgot
forgive	forgave	forgiven
forsake	forsook	forsaken
freeze	froze	frozen
get	got	got *or* gotten
gild	gilt	gilt
gird	girded	girded *or* girt
give	gave	given
go	went	gone
grind	ground	ground
grow	grew	grown
hang	hung	hung
have has	had	had
hear	heard	heard
heave	heaved *or* hove (*old-fashioned*)	heaved
hew	hewed	hewn *or* hewed
hide	hid	hidden *or* hid
hit	hit	hit
hold	held	held
hurt	hurt	hurt
keep	kept	kept
kneel	knelt *or* kneeled	knelt
knit	knitted *or* knit	knitted *or* knit
know	knew	known
lade	laded	laded *or* laden
lay	laid	laid
lead	led	led
lean	leant *or* leaned	leant *or* leaned
leap	leapt *or* leaped	leapt *or* leaped

Infinitive	Past Tense	Past Participle
learn	learnt *or* learned	learnt *or* learned
leave	left	left
lend	lent	lent
let	let	let
lie	lay	lain
light	lit *or* lighted	lit *or* lighted
lose	lost	lost
make	made	made
Pres. Indic. may	might	–
mean	meant	meant
meet	met	met
mistake	mistook	mistaken
mow	mowed	mowed *or* mown
Pres. Indic. must	–	–
pay	paid	paid
put	put	put
quit	quitted *or* quit	quitted *or* quit
read	read	read
rend	rent	rent
rid	rid	rid
ride	rode	ridden
ring	rang	rung
rise	rose	risen
rive	rived	riven *or* rived
run	ran	run
saw	sawed	sawn
say	said	said
see	saw	seen
seek	sought	sought
sell	sold	sold
send	sent	sent
set	set	set
shake	shook	shaken
Pres. Indic. shall	should	–
shear	sheared	sheared *or* shorn
shed	shed	shed
shew	shewed	shewn *or* shewed
shine	shone	shone
shoe	shod	shod
shoot	shot	shot
show	showed	shown *or* showed
shrink	shrank *or* shrunk	shrunk *or* shrunken
shrive	shrove	shriven
shut	shut	shut
sing	sang	sung
sink	sank	sunk *or* sunken
sit	sat	sat
slay	slew	slain
sleep	slept	slept

Infinitive	Past Tense	Past Participle
slide	slid	slid
sling	slung	slung
slink	slunk	slunk
slit	slit	slit
smell	smelt *or* smelled	smelt *or* smelled
smite	smote	smitten
sow	sowed	sown *or* sowed
speak	spoke	spoken
speed	sped *or* speeded	sped *or* speeded
spell	spelt *or* spelled	spelt *or* spelled
spend	spent	spent
spill	spilt *or* spilled	spilt *or* spilled
spin	spun	spun
spit	spat	spat
split	split	split
spoil	spoilt *or* spoiled	spoilt *or* spoiled
spread	spread	spread
spring	sprang	sprung
stand	stood	stood
stave	staved *or* stove	staved *or* stove
steal	stole	stolen
stick	stuck	stuck
sting	stung	stung
stink	stank	stunk
strew	strewed	strewed *or* strewn
stride	strode	stridden
strike	struck	struck *or* stricken
string	strung	strung
strive	strove	striven
swear	swore	sworn
sweep	swept	swept
swell	swelled	swollen *or* swelled
swim	swam	swum
swing	swung	swung
take	took	taken
teach	taught	taught
tear	tore	torn
tell	told	told
think	thought	thought
thrive	thrived *or* throve	thrived *or* thriven
throw	threw	thrown
thrust	thrust	thrust
tread	trod	trodden
understand	understood	understood
undo	undid	undone
upset	upset	upset
wake	woke *or* waked	waked *or* woken
wear	wore	worn
weave	wove	woven
weep	wept	wept

Infinitive	Past Tense	Past Participle
wet	wetted *or* wet	wetted *or* wet
will	would	–
win	won	won
wind	wound	wound
withdraw	withdrew	withdrawn
withstand	withstood	withstood
wring	wrung	wrung
write	wrote	written

Index

Note: words whose usage is discussed in the text are listed in the index in *italic type*.